The Journey of Josephine

The Doll That Mended A Broken Heart

Bambi Lynn

Book Cover by Amber Mathwich (author's daughter)

Edited by Joy Melody

1st edition 2023

Dedications

In seventh and eighth grade I had an English teacher named Miss Ludwig who believed in me. She called me into her office one day and said, "Bambi, you have a gift, and one day you are going to use that gift and write a book."

Well, Miss Ludwig, you were right. It's finally happened.

I dedicate this book to the only six people that will ever call me Mom! My heart is full of the many cherished moments I have had with each of you. You are my greatest loves. As your lives continue to unfold, my wish is that you pursue your dreams. And when the chance arises…

I hope you dance.

I also dedicate this book to the one and only true God that took the hurts of a little girl and molded her into something beautiful!

Editor's Introduction

by Joy Melody

If you've lived long enough to be interested in reading a book with content like this one, you're familiar with life-altering moments… those moments that appear in a historical timeline or would have been etched onto Moses's staff. If Bambi's life was laid out on a long sheet of parchment or carved into wood or stone, the words "Christmas 1976" and "Josephine Priscilla" would most definitely be there.

Although this is her story, there was life before Josephine… a life that little rag doll was designed, cut, and stitched for and gifted into. In keeping with the author's wishes to start Chapter 1 of this story with Josephine's arrival, she has given me permission to set the stage here. That stage is filled with lots of other smaller, but still significant, moments. Those moments influenced the lens by which Bambi viewed and interpreted the world around her.

Bambi did not see her world as being very safe. It was, however, predictable… predictably chaotic. "Home" was synonymous with never knowing what to expect the next moment. It was longing for love, acceptance, nurture and protection from those you also feared and could not depend on. When a child's formative years are like this, times and places can all seem to blend together. Days, months and years are hard to separate because they all hold the same feeling of *fear*... in the same setting of *chaos*.

Memories don't attach according to a timeline when trauma is present. For instance, Bambi doesn't remember specifically when her dad lived with them and when he didn't or how often he was gone versus present. But she does remember that at one point he drove a big semi-truck that transported cars and at some point the family traveled with him. As the smallest of the children, Bambi had to sit on the floor of the passenger's side of the semi's cab between her mom's legs. One time they had lunch around some huge logs and then slept overnight in the cars that were on the trailer.

Most of Bambi's memories of her dad were far more traumatic. He was a drunk … and a mean one. One time he got so drunk that all the children hid in the bathtub together. They could hear their dad trying to pick up the refrigerator and then hitting their mother. The police came that time. Episodes like this were just part of the cycle of Bambi's mom and the kids escaping to Grandma's house, Mom finding them a new place to live without Dad, Dad getting sober, Mom taking Dad back, Dad starting to drink again, and Mom needing to run with them again.

Bambi assumes that her dad was sent to rehab on occasion. But her only actual memory of him being somewhere that could be a rehab is attached to remembering the first time she smelled a skunk. It's the distinct memory of when she discovered the putrid aroma that triggers the place- a red building with the skunk under its porch stairs- and the reason for being there- to visit her dad inside, sitting at a round table. The memory is not attached to spending time with her father or why or how she felt about it. Rather, it is attached to what she felt and thought about the skunk.

You, the reader, will find many similar examples within the following pages. Parts of this story will be eloquently communicated while others will not contain perfectly smooth writing. You may notice repetition in descriptions. That is because much of this story includes repeated trauma. You will be taken along the same path, with the same feelings and thoughts the author experienced, both in the living and in the reminiscing and retelling. There might be questions left unaddressed.

Sometimes information is left out or altered slightly in sensitivity to, or in protection of, others' privacy. Sometimes her brain has protected Bambi's inner child, and specific memories or timelines aren't accessible to her. Sometimes information that is irrelevant to Josephine's journey has been left out to avoid distraction. All this is part of the bittersweet beauty of joining *Bambi's journey*, from *Bambi's perspective*, and with *Bambi's repercussions*.

Her memories were filed as either singularly *good* or *bad* moments. For instance, there is a memory of a rented house with a barn that held pigs and a vegetable garden. That sounds lovely, right? But it was not so for Bambi...

One day Bambi caught her brother, who had many food allergies, out in the yard eating peas or beans off the vine from that garden. In trying to protect him the best she knew how, she told him he could die from eating them and to put them down. Bambi's brother started crying and ran in the house.

When her dad saw that his son was upset, he asked him why. Her brother repeated what she had said. Bambi's father screamed for her to come to where he was sitting on the couch in the living room. When she complied he pulled off his belt, told her to never talk about his son that way, and beat her so badly that she could barely walk at school the following days. Bambi's mother was there, just sitting in her chair where she had been knitting.

While Bambi's mom was clearly too afraid of her husband to intervene with his *discipline* of his daughter, her fear was not isolated to him. She herself had never had a positive example of how to mother. Now she found herself in survival mode, with kids in tow. In an attempt to protect her children from having the same things happen to them as happened to her, she parented out of fear and tried to keep her children in a confined bubble.

By the time Bambi's mom left her dad for the last time, she was a broken shell of a woman and mother. There was no ability left in her to nurture, and so she did the only thing she understood. She feared and she attempted to control her children. Bambi and her sister were not allowed to go to school dances or basketball games. When they snuck to a game, her mom showed up and dragged them home. Makeup was also not allowed. When caught wearing it, Bambi's mom slapped her across the face in front of all her friends.

It wasn't until Bambi's 30th high school class reunion that she fully realized the extent of the "globe" she and her siblings lived inside while her classmates, in Bambi's words, "lived life" *normally* all around her. Bambi's classmates talked about sledding and ice-skating, and at first she assumed it was in a different place. She had no idea that such opportunities and adventures existed and had happened *locally*. Bambi had grown up inside that globe while everyone else was right outside, seemingly living a fuller life.

It was the stifling control, fueled by fear, which caused Bambi and her sister to start sneaking out of the house when her mom was gone at work. It was her mom's need to feel in control of something, anything, that caused her to control what little she could… like restricting heat, water, shampoo and conditioner, withholding what their landline phone number was so friends could not call, and requiring Bambi to work and give her the earnings.

The way Bambi sees it, instead of acknowledging her fear, her mom chose to choke her children's lives. And then Bambi ended up no different. There was the generational issue of marital abuse and codependency. And out of her own fear, Bambi went to the other extreme of making everything about her kids and a grand finale of life. In not wanting her kids to ever feel choked by neglect and lack, she ended up choking them with an overabundance of attention, hovering, and adventures. This realization has helped Bambi in forgiving her mother as well as having compassion for her own children as they process their childhoods.

Forgiveness is such an interesting concept…

Bambi and I became friends and bonded over our similar accounts of escaping marital abuse. And let me tell you, there is a whole lot to forgive our ex-spouses for. I have discovered that it's a whole lot easier when I look at my ex not as the man he pretended or promised to be, or as the man I tried to love, serve, or pray him into becoming, but as the man he actually *is*. It doesn't leave much to forgive when a person is just being *who they are*. Forgiveness is replaced with acceptance. And whatever I can accept as reality, I have no need to forgive. I just simply accept its truth.

It was Bambi's desire that in this space, before and outside of her story where the raw facts of her mother's flaws are further exposed in detail, I add an element of her humanity. And in doing so, you, the reader, are hopefully released to feel grace and mercy towards her, to better understand and accept her as she is. It's my honor to attempt to do just that. Let's begin here:

Bambi's mom only allowed each child two sets of clothes to be worn to school in any given week (one on Monday, Wednesday and Friday, the other on Tuesday and Thursday) in order to conserve on laundry. Baths were allowed once a week and shared with siblings to conserve on hot water. It was a heavy weight to carry the stigma, week after week and year after year, of being known as the dirty kids who wore the same clothes.

And yet, Bambi's mom somehow found the time and resources to make extra hats and gloves for them. While she didn't know how, or didn't have the ability, to meet her children's everyday physical needs or emotionally nurture them, she was indulgent in other areas that were priorities to her. For instance, every year Bambi and her sister received a different kind of homemade doll from their mother for Christmas. One year it was a crocheted doll that fit over an empty bleach bottle to hold its form. Another year it was made of porcelain with a fine dress. And then there was the year of Josephine Priscilla, the rag doll. Investing in the time and money to create all these things tapped into something Bambi's mother *did* know how to do… knit, crochet and sew.

I imagine her mom working on those hats, gloves, and dolls as a coping mechanism. They were her priorities because they helped hold her sanity together. Where she couldn't control what happened to herself, her children, or, to a degree, how good or nurturing of a mother she was able to be, she at least could knit yarn into gloves that warmed a child's hands she did not clasp. Stitch by stitch, she could create a rag doll that would hold her daughter's heart's broken pieces in a way she could not, would not.

I have found myself many times during this editing process reflecting on how, out of all the other different dolls Bambi received for Christmases, none compared to Josephine. She was the only one, out of all the dolls Bambi's mother made over the years, which she kept. For some reason Bambi just connected with her. That could partly be because the rag doll was the only one she could carry around freely, as the others weren't made to play with. Those others could be viewed as more *valuable*… but they were also more *fragile* and *impractical*.

Before we go any further, I encourage you to take a moment to look at the front cover photo of this book. Look at Josephine. Imagine for a moment what she looked like brand new. Now wonder with me how she got to look the way she does now… Isn't she beautiful? … In spite of… or maybe because of… her raggedness?

The meaning behind the name that Bambi gave this rag doll is something to keep in mind as this story unfolds. Josephine means "Jehovah increases" or "He shall increase." It's also the feminine of Joseph. His Bible story is one of abandonment, rejection, of literally being thrown away and discarded over and over (first into a well and then into prison), and yet God used each event, over and over, to bring increase to Joseph's life (and eventually to his entire family)!

Priscilla means "ancient, venerable, deserving a great deal of honor and respect, especially because of age, wisdom or character, admirable, esteemed, revered." In the Bible she is often thought to have been the first example of a female preacher/teacher in early church history.

As you begin the unfolding of this bittersweet story, as you discover the purpose of this rag doll, as you witness the surviving and thriving of Bambi's life… *in spite of*… I pray you experience the same inspiration, the same hope, as I felt. Enjoy the discovery, amidst the heartaches and tears, of how a mother's weak, alternative gift of a doll, in replacement of the maternal support she could not provide, *stood in the gap.*

Welcome to **The Journey of Josephine**, the story of how God used a rag doll, whose name represents His provision and increase in spite of repeated brokenness, to mend a broken heart. Discover how that mended heart now resembles the biblical Priscilla.

We all have hearts in need of mending. May this story become part of your story, part of your mending. And may you find *your name*…

1

I never would have thought that a Christmas present to a six-year-old little girl would give her healing throughout her life. How could a small rag doll be something that brings joy to me still, even in my 50s? I don't think my mom would've imagined that those long hours of putting that doll together would be something that continued to hold me together so many years later. I can only imagine the hours that she spent piecing all the fabrics together, stuffing her in all the right places, and using just enough stuffing to make her form. How could I have known when I saw that rag doll for the first time, as the wrapping paper was torn away from her, that she would so often mend my pieces, holding me together?

In 1979 a movie came out called Orphan Train about children in New York City that were without families. Although it's now old, it still blesses my heart. I watched it the other day and cried tears until I couldn't cry any more. One of the characters was a little girl that was abandoned by her mom because the woman's boyfriend didn't want the burden of taking care of a child. In desperation, she dressed up as a boy and called herself 'JP' so she could survive by selling newspapers. A mission home decided to collect and take orphaned children from the city out west on a train to give them families and homes. It was revealed on the train that JP was really a girl named Josephine Priscilla.

When I was a little girl I watched this movie and decided to name my rag doll after that orphaned girl, which is so bizarre to me thinking about it now. I didn't really understand what an orphan was but knew it was somebody that didn't belong anywhere or to anybody. An orphan was somebody that nobody wanted, someone who had to beg for a place in somebody's heart. I often felt this way throughout my life.

But my Josephine Priscilla was never an orphan to me. She was loved and carried from place to place throughout all of my years and sits on my dresser still today as a reminder that God used a present on Christmas Day to help me throughout the years. She was a present that kept on giving in the darkest moments of my life.

She looks really raggedy today as if she's been through some stuff… a dark journey. Her journey wasn't easy, as you can see from her rips and tears and the stains from my dirty hands that have touched her face. She has lost some of her clothing. And yet, she looks more put together every time I look at her. Maybe that's because she's helped put and keep me together all these years. She taught me that I was never alone. All this… from a little rag doll received on Christmas Day.

The earliest recollection that I have of Josephine Priscilla giving me comfort was, oddly enough, while spending the night at my grandparents' house. I had always loved being at my grandma's house. It always seemed like a safe place for me, so different than the chaotic home that

I lived in. When I went there it was peaceful, a place where I sat on the couch and the stillness alone brought that feeling of safety.

My grandma always made things special with a breakfast of Apple Jacks cereal and toast with various homemade jellies. My favorite was peach. She had orange juice and, we could always have two cookies for a treat. Sometimes they were chocolate chip and sometimes they were peanut butter. I loved grandma so very much.

I never knew my grandma's first husband, my mom's dad. She married the jolly, heavyset, balding man that I knew as Grandpa before I was born. He always sat in the same chair in the living room watching the news on the console TV.

At bedtime I got to sleep in my Uncle Timmy's room. They always called it Timmy's Room because there was a Patrick's Room too. These were my uncles, but they didn't live there anymore. Uncle Patrick had passed away when I was a little girl. Uncle Timmy got married, and I only have vague memories of him. But whenever I got to stay at my grandma's house, I got to sleep in that big bed in Uncle Timmy's room all by myself. This was a big deal since I shared a bed with my sister when I was at home.

Before bedtime, my grandma would start the shower for me to make sure that I was nice and clean for when I put my pajamas on. She always had Dove soap, and I can still smell that amazing aroma even today. She had a really nice shower, which was very important to me because we didn't have a shower at my house. We had a claw-foot bathtub where my sister and I shared a bath once a week. Mom would wash our hair for our weekly ritual of preparing ourselves for the coming week of school.

Compared to my home, having a shower all by myself was amazing. Then Grandma would tuck me into bed where the sheets were always clean and crisp. She was the one that taught me how to make a bed and to make things look so pretty. This is a habit that I still carry on today.

Then something happened… I was awakened in the middle of the night by my grandfather. It seemed really weird that he was in my room. I didn't understand why! He had a bathrobe on, and I remember opening my eyes just a little bit. For some reason my mind and my body started racing and I was really scared.

My grandfather untied his bathrobe and his private parts were right near me. Then he purposely put his penis on my leg. I pretended I was sleeping because I didn't know if I was doing something wrong. Would somebody blame me, a little girl, for my grandfather coming into the room and taking my innocence away? I kept that secret for a very long time, until the day my grandmother died.

I also remember a night that, for some reason, I wasn't sleeping in the Uncle Timmy Room. Maybe somebody was there for Christmas or another holiday. I ended up sleeping in between my grandma and grandpa in their bed. My grandfather touched me in the middle of the night in my private parts. Being a little girl, I couldn't understand my current feelings, much less comprehend the future implications.

For the rest of my life I have had dreams of those two moments and wondered if I made them up in my head.

Looking back to that time seems really weird to me. To this day, I still feel uncomfortable when I hear of grandparents having their grandchildren sleep in bed with them. It makes me feel uneasy.

For a long time I tried to convince myself that maybe it was my sister that this happened to and I just couldn't see it. Besides, I loved my grandma so much. I wasn't willing to tell her what had happened and lose the chance of being able to stay overnight or have Apple Jacks cereal, jam on my toast or orange juice for breakfast. I didn't want to lose the opportunity to take a shower with Dove soap and to be with my grandma as she taught me how to clean and bake and even how to can. Most precious of all, she told me that I was important, and I could not risk losing that and not having her in my life.

If anybody ever found out about those encounters with my grandfather, I somehow knew I wouldn't be able to go back there. So I told the only one who could keep the secret, my Josephine Priscilla. I knew that she would never tell anybody. She understood my fear that if anybody was to ever find out what he did, everybody would be mad at me. So I squeezed my rag doll so tightly and told her never to tell anybody and that the secret would be hers and mine. It would be one of those secrets that Josephine Priscilla would keep forever, that she would never tell anybody. She always handled my squeeze hugs and my tears falling on her face.

After my grandma died I told the family what my grandfather had done because that secret didn't only happen to me but to others in my family as well. I just couldn't be the one to say anything when my grandma was alive. So my rag doll and I would stick together and we would heal with each other. I could trust Josephine. She really was one of my best friends. She kept all my secrets.

When you live in a chaotic household where you never know what each day will bring and how each day will end, you create something that becomes real to you and brings comfort. Sometimes people have their thumb, a special blankie, or toy, but I had Josephine. My escape from an unstable reality, she was something I could trust, and that never changed. Always there for me, she never spoke back, didn't demand all the attention, and never disciplined me for a wrong word or how I said something. She never belittled, made fun of me when I walked into a room, or said things that could never be taken back. My rag doll never hit me with a belt and left bruises on my back because of something that I did because I was just a child. She never told me she hated me or that I didn't belong. A comfort in the darkest of moments, she brought safety to me.

Josephine Priscilla became my escape from the reality of my life, from the screaming and yelling of an alcoholic father. I never had to cover my ears around her because she was going to say something so mean that I would remember into my adult life. She never said I was stupid or ugly or an unwanted little girl. When those terrible words were spoken over me, she blessed me with her presence. She brought security to the insecure world that I was living in behind the closed doors of my home. I escaped into a fantasy world with my best friend, my rag doll.

2

I distinctly remember being told that we were going to move to Virginia because my dad had gone through rehab and wasn't drinking anymore. He had found Jesus at his Southern Baptist church and wanted a chance for his family to be together again. Dad wanted a chance to not have alcohol be his bondage and source of comfort. He held down a job for a little while and was trying to prove to my mom that we needed to be a family.

My mom took my brothers and sister and I and moved to Virginia. I lost the haven of my grandma living across the street. I lost having extended family living next door and cousins that we played with all the time. Now we would have to find new friends. We would have to find a new normal as our normal had been ripped from us.

It took me a lot of years to forgive my mom for moving us back with my dad. I was so apprehensive at the time, remembering the abuse, the screaming, and the not feeling safe. But my mom said that marriage deserves a second chance. I didn't understand this concept until I was in abusive relationships myself and found myself giving chance after chance too.

I don't hate my mom anymore for her decision. As a mother myself, I understand her trying really hard to make decisions that kept her family together. But as an 8-

year-old little girl I was furious and scared. I was scared of living with somebody that I knew didn't like me, and I never could figure out the reason why. I was scared of my dad stumbling into the house looking for more money so he could buy more beer. I was scared of his belt and the noise of the belt coming off of his pants. I was scared of not having my grandma across the street from me. However, as a little girl, this wasn't my decision to make. I had to go along with the choices that my parents made. It was my responsibility to just obey and to listen.

The first few months living with my dad were great. He went to church with us and sang "The Old Rugged Cross" in front of the whole congregation. He was able to hold a job. There was no longer physical abuse and no kids running to hide underneath the ironing board so he wouldn't see us (Mom wasn't a good housekeeper and it was left up all the time). There was no longer hiding to avoid him lining us up on the couch to tell us once again that he wasn't my father, that he hated me, and that I didn't belong to him. For a little while I didn't have to hear that I specifically wasn't his daughter. It was almost normal. I was almost happy.

I wish I could say that it ended well, but it didn't. My dad started drinking away his paycheck again, stumbling into the house on a Friday afternoon with no money left. Mom started trying to find jobs. The screaming and yelling began again. I don't remember ever feeling safe.

Those two years spent in Virginia were hell. I thought there was never going to be an escape. Once again I clung to my rag doll. I clung to her tighter because I was afraid that something could happen to her and I would not have my safety, my escape from reality, and my help through those dark nights.

When your mind cannot comprehend what is going on, it shuts down and different parts of your brain forget moments. My mind didn't know how to deal with such trauma, so it hid itself. It couldn't handle remembering all the truths, all the pieces, and so it shut down. I wish I could remember so much more than I do from back then, but I think it was my mind's way of allowing me to heal. Maybe those moments were too painful for me and my mind was protecting me.

I think that children that go through trauma have to have a pretend life, something to hang onto, because how could they survive the real one if they didn't? I believe some imaginary friends come from these dark moments. You imagine you have a best friend, somebody that rides and dies with you. You make up a friend that really likes you, and you sit up late into the night telling each other secrets. Sadly, you wake up in the morning and realize it was all pretend. But that little break from reality helps you survive another day.

After two years my mom came up with a plan to pack up our stuff and move back to my grandma's house where things seemed a little more normal. We would move back to our little town and once again start all over. My mom would find a job and a place for us to call home.

These were years of poverty in many ways. My mom worked overnight from 11 p.m. to 7 a.m., leaving us alone at the ages of 11, 10, 8, and 5. She slept during the day and found ways for us to stay out of her hair. Most days we rode our bikes miles away to a summer community park program she'd paid for us to attend. We stayed from early morning until dinner time so that we wouldn't disturb her sleeping.

Being in the house wasn't a place that I felt safe or nurtured anyway. To prevent our friends from calling us, we weren't allowed to know our own phone number. My brother was angry and would wrestle and tickle me until I peed. It never seemed like there was any other choice but to be outside the entire day. We all made the best of it! If we weren't at the park we were playing in the woods, making forts, having walnut wars in the baseball field, or playing badminton in the front yard for hours on end.

I think my mom *wanted* to love us, but I didn't *feel* loved. My grandma hadn't become nurturing until her older years, so she was different when raising my mom compared to how loving she was with me. Besides not having had a loving, motherly role to model after, my mom was consumed with so much hurt and pain from the abuse that she endured from my father. I don't think she had the skills, time, or energy to find ways to love us. She was just surviving, and thus so were we.

My mother's fear overtook rationality. There were really cold nights with only a kerosene heater because she didn't want to turn the heat on. We weren't allowed to use the water when she wasn't at home. The water would be turned off, and shampoo and conditioner would be hidden.

There were a lot of chores, with us kids pretty much taking care of the house. However, our cleanliness was not a priority. There weren't nice baths or showers every night like at grandma's house. But there would be a Sunday night bath time, sharing the tub with my sister while mother oversaw washing our hair. This continued until I was around 14 years old. To clean the few outfits we had for school, I took the family's clothes to the laundromat and hung them on the line in our backyard. I would take a wagon into town and bring the wagon back. We looked at it as torture, but she probably looked at it as saving money.

3

When I was thirteen I started working, paying my mom half of everything that I made, but still wasn't allowed to use the water. I babysat three kids for 75 cents an hour and picked strawberries. My next job was babysitting a woman with dementia while her family went out to auctions every Saturday. They paid me three dollars an hour, which was pretty good money. This benefitted my family, but for me it came with a cost! The woman's son, a dirty old man, would come get me every Saturday in a big white Buick car. I didn't know it then, but now that I am older and know my cars a little better, I know it was a Buick. For years seeing a white Buick still triggered me.

He didn't do anything to me at first but would just tell me how pretty I was. Then every Saturday morning he would get a little bit friskier and handsy. He began by just touching my leg, and I would freeze because I didn't know what to do. I would nudge myself closer to the door so he couldn't reach me and then run into his house to where the lady was. I would beg my mom to let me walk home every Saturday afternoon, but she wouldn't let me.

I would tell her that I didn't want to work for them anymore, and she told me that wasn't a choice, that I was making money and I was giving her half of it. She didn't know that the dirty old man was putting his fingers into my pants and arousing a 13-year-old girl that was still playing with Barbies. I just wanted to find a way to get out of his white Buick, away from his dirty fingers, but I was paralyzed.

At night I would hold my rag doll and tell her how dirty I felt and that I just wanted to scream for him to just leave me alone. I secretly plotted with her that I would start wearing pants so he wouldn't be able to put his fingers through. It helped for a little while, but then he still found a way.

Every time I drive through my hometown and see that house on the corner it still makes me cringe. The place brings me back to the moment where a dirty old man decided to take my innocence, making my body feel a way that I had never experienced. My body was awakened at thirteen in ways that stole my childhood.

The only one I confided in, the only one who ever knew the secret of what went on, was Josephine Priscilla. She was the only one that knew my dirty secret of taking twenties out of his wallet whenever it sat out on the table. It was his punishment, a way I could spite him for what he was stealing from me. I shared my tears with Josephine, and she never asked me questions that I didn't have answers to.

She couldn't make me feel safe anymore, but she did make me feel like I had somebody to tell. I wish I could've stood up to that dirty man, but that would mean telling someone besides Josephine. And I was convinced that nobody would have ever believed me and I would have lost my job. I don't know if I would make a different decision even now, as the price of telling would have been so high. I felt obligated to help my mom, and that meant getting into that white Buick every Saturday and keeping that secret.

That secret was the starting point in my journey of destruction. I began to doubt myself and to not feel innocent anymore. That secret made me feel dirty, and I needed to find a way to wash it away. I didn't know if telling Josephine my secrets could really help me anymore. It was never that she wasn't constant in my life. It was just that her knowing my secrets wasn't taking any of the pain away anymore.

I couldn't get a grip on life or figure out how to make the pain inside of me go away. There was nothing to latch on to that would make me feel special. I couldn't take away the chaos that lingered in my head and in my thoughts. I just wanted to run away from it all. At the time I didn't understand that it was an issue of not feeling loved or safe. Where could I go that I felt safe, that I belonged? Where could I go that somebody wasn't going to hurt me, make me feel unworthy?

That day came in the form of a pill. I started taking these little black pills that somebody gave me in school. I started vomiting and keeping track of the foods that went down my throat. I had to find a way to take control of my own body. It doesn't make sense now because vomiting or taking pills and then taking laxatives wasn't making me feel better. What I was trying to control was actually controlling me.

At the time I didn't understand how the mind plays tricks on you as it's trying to figure out the chaos. I just kept taking those little pills and vomiting in the toilets. I just continued keeping the secrets. I had so many secrets and no place to go and nobody to tell them to. That's where Josephine had always come to the rescue. But as my childhood was disappearing and innocence was unraveling, so was her power to comfort me.

I could see that my brain was spiraling. I tried to run away several times but didn't know where to go. I would just walk the streets in town and end up coming back because there was nowhere else to go. I could be found at my grandma's house, and I surely didn't want to get her in trouble for housing a fugitive like me. But I just wanted the pain to stop. I wanted all the secrets that I had told my rag doll to not have to be secrets anymore. I wanted to be able to dream of something better but didn't even know how to dream. How do you dream when life is so different than your dreams? I just wanted to be liked, to belong, and I didn't want to have any more pain.

Age thirteen was the first time that I ever thought of suicide. It was just a thought, nothing that I acted on, because I wouldn't know how to do it anyhow. I was just tired. I was tired of the pain that was within my home. I was tired of being bullied at school. I was tired of the chaos of the outside world and the chaos within the walls of my home. How could I get it all to stop? How could I find peace? Did it really exist? Or was this all that life had to offer? I think back to those years and don't even remember thinking that I would grow up into adulthood, to where things could be different.

There didn't seem to be a way out of my house of chaos. I didn't know how to stop believing the things that people were telling me or how to look beyond the present and into a future that could possibly be better. Any concept of dreaming or having hope of something different did not exist. I didn't know I could be someone other than the character I was playing within my mother's world. I didn't know that growing up meant getting to choose who I wanted to be, do what I wanted to do.

I was bullied a lot at school, not that bullying didn't happen to everybody, but being named Bambi and being poor seemed to make it worse. I just had to live moment by moment through the pain and the rejection. Somehow the moments became days, and the days became years. Someday there would come a moment when I would just burst and know that this is the day that I would leave and everything would be better. Until that day I just continued to live life, to just cry out for some kind of love and for somebody to notice that I was alive.

I finally started developing at 15 years old and won the attention of guys that were older than me. They were out of school and drove up and down my road and around the main streets in their nice cars. I would walk down my street in cute little shorts enjoying the honks of the horn and the attention that I was getting. This was attention that I wanted and not that somebody was demanding *from* me. I was seeking the attention to see if I was really somebody that a male would actually want to be with and not just force himself upon.

I had my first sexual encounter with somebody I liked that was a lot older than me. It was the kind of crush that you have on a teen star and get his poster to hang in your room. One day my sister and I were walking up and down the street. My crush and his friend pulled over on the side of the road and started talking to us. We were really giddy because these were really popular guys and they stopped to talk to *us*. They asked if we wanted to meet up with them at night. That would mean sneaking out of the house and running down the street to get into their car to drive off. But for some reason my sister and I said yes. We were up for the adventure. I had no idea what the adventure was going to be but knew this guy that I'd had a crush on forever asked me to get into his car secretly, and that made it so enticing. If I would've only known what was going to happen.

We went to their house and downstairs in the basement. The basement was redone and was really nice. They brought out some wine, and my sister and I drank it along with them. The one guy took my sister into one room, and this guy and I sat on the couch together. I honestly can say that I don't know how anything happened. But we had sex, and it was my first time. It wasn't anything great or magical, I don't think. It just was...
I didn't know what sex was supposed to be like when you had a crush on somebody and him on you. So I didn't even know what to expect.

All I remember clearly is that we got back into their car, they drove us home, and my sister and I snuck back into our house. The next day my sister went around telling everybody in the school what happened. The bullying got even worse than it ever was before because people didn't believe what my sister was saying. I felt so much pain, though, that I knew that it had happened. I couldn't walk right and was bleeding.

That encounter, along with finding out a little while later that my crush got married and was expecting a child, set me on a spiral out of control. The nine months following the incident were spent in the backseat of cars, buses, yards, people's houses and boats. As "Bambi, the poor girl," I was not pursued by any of the boys from my high school. These others were young men but older than me, and anywhere they wanted to take me, I went. Nothing ever felt like love, and everything always felt like emptiness. It wasn't like they called me and wanted me to be their girlfriend. It was more that this girl was willing and so they were able to take advantage.

I wish I could understand what was going through my head at that time in my life. Why was I doing what I was doing? I was having secret conversations with my rag doll, but she never answered me back. She never told me that I was trying to look for some kind of love. She never reminded me of my worth and the value that I had within me. She never reminded me that I had a purpose and that one day I would walk in it. She just listened like she always did, and that helped me walk through the stage.

I knew something had to give. Something drastic had to happen in my life. I knew that all the secrets that were bottling up were going to make me burst one day. But how could I get it to stop? I made a plan to go live with my uncle who was divorced from my dad's sister. I secretly packed my bags and hid them under my bed until the moment that I would say goodbye and start living a better life.

4

I chose my sixteenth birthday. I wanted so badly to have a birthday party, but it was something that my mother wasn't having. I wanted something that everybody else at school could have, like a sleepover party with some friends. Every year my mom made an angel food cake, and I just wanted a store-bought cake this time. My mom told me I was spoiled and that she was not going to give me a party. I knew at that moment that I was done.

I knew that I would get into my uncle's car the next day, drive off to a new school, and start a new life. I wasn't going to have to keep any more secrets. With all my belongings, including my rag doll, in a garbage bag, I walked out of the door, hoping to never return. I didn't know what I had gotten myself into, and at that moment I didn't care. It was the closest thing to freedom that I had ever experienced. I thought I was feeling independence and that now I was going to run my life with my own rules. The prospect of going to a new school felt like I was on top of the world. I was a little scared that my mother would come after me and drag me back home, but at that moment I didn't care. The next day that car door closed and I was on my way.

I had my own room. The room had bunk beds, so I slept on the bottom. I didn't have a lot of belongings but of what I had, I put my clothes in the dresser drawers, set my things on top of the dresser, put my bed together and put my rag doll in the corner of my bed.

The first couple of months were amazing. I went to a new school and had my first real boyfriend. He held my hand through classes, and I showed him off in the school halls. My uncle entered me into the teen beauty pageant at my new high school. I earned scholarships to take modeling classes and build a portfolio. He encouraged it as well as bought me nice clothes and allowed me to have the boyfriend. I didn't see the premeditated grooming of his actions at the time, but in hindsight that is what he was doing.

It didn't take long for things to get awkward. While I was sleeping, my uncle would come into my room with a flashlight and just stare at me. We would have weird conversations at the table. He would ask me strange things that I didn't think you should ever ask a young girl. He made me feel so uncomfortable, doing things like walking into the bathroom while I was taking a shower, making excuses that he didn't know I was in there. He would want to rub my back while I was sitting on the couch. I would always tell him no and get up and walk away.

He had a security system that went off in his room if I unlocked and opened the windows in my bedroom. I would have private conversations on the phone, and he would later ask me questions that he could only know if he had been listening in. He was somehow recording and listening to my conversations. I couldn't tell anybody because I had just left my mother's house, and now here I was in a house that I didn't feel safe. I felt uneasy and scared all the time.

Then the weirdness and the uneasiness began to really get out of control. One time I was sleeping on the couch, waiting for my clothes to get done in the washing machine so I could move them into the dryer. I must've just dozed off when my uncle came over and sat down on the couch, put his hands in my pants, and started rubbing my genitals. I just kept my eyes closed. I was so scared that if I moved something terrible would happen to me. So I froze.

I wish my body hadn't frozen, hadn't reacted to his gross touch. I didn't know what was going on and didn't know what I was feeling, but I knew I was mad because it was another dirty old man that had his fingers in my pants and I couldn't stop it. I couldn't even open up my eyes by that point because fear had taken over.

I remember hearing the beep of the washing machine and thinking I needed to get up, but I didn't know how. My uncle stopped what he was doing and said, "Well somebody liked that," and walked away as if nothing had ever happened. I didn't know how to get up, much less how to process what had just happened. If I was to run, where would I go? I was more scared than I had ever been but didn't know how to process that fear. So I filed that incident in the back of my head and walked around as if nothing ever happened… until it happened again and again and again.

I tried to sneak out at night, but the windows would beep. Every night I would switch around what bed I slept on. I thought if I tricked him he wouldn't continue to play this game with me, and then he would just leave me alone. So some nights I would sleep on the top bunk and then would switch which end the pillow was at. And other nights I would sleep on the bottom bunk and switch back and forth. But the abuse didn't stop.

I cried myself to sleep every night and went to school feeling numb each morning. I couldn't even tell my boyfriend because he was really good friends with my family, including being best friends with my cousin. His parents were straight from Korea, and the difference in culture added to my not feeling like I could tell him that I had an uncle that was abusing me. How could anybody, much less he and his very conservative, private family understand?

One night it got so bad that I put a plastic bag over my head and held it really tightly on my neck, hoping that my uncle wouldn't come into my room until I was gone, until my last breath had been taken. I wanted so badly to be left alone and just die. I thought that bag over my head would bring me freedom. But instead I began to gasp. He came into my room, took the bag off, turned around, and left again. Why couldn't I have just died at that very moment? I took my doll from the corner of my bed and cried with her in my arms. Once again it was the nearness of Josephine, my rag doll, which allowed me to cry myself to sleep as my tears fell on her face.

My mom started coming around after that day. I'm not sure whether it was really to visit me or facilitated by my uncle to manipulate her. There had been a strange connection between them for years, but nobody could ever pinpoint what was going on. I knew there was some kind of relationship, but none of us could figure out what kind of relationship they had. She came around more often but never asked or begged me to make a different decision about coming home. She was just around more.

The abuse didn't end. He got more manipulating and calculated. There were subtle comments made and threats like "I have pictures of you" and "How did your panties get in my room?" The things he said were really strange, and I walked around in fear. I didn't know what my next move was going to be, but I was either going to die or escape. Either way, a decision had to be made.

I walked by the nurse counselor at school many times thinking that if I just went in there and told her maybe she could stop the abuse that was going on in that home. But then my uncle started showing up to the school randomly. It was like he was watching me and knew my every move. I couldn't escape the glare of his eyes and the smirk that was always on his face. I knew what fear was now even more than I'd ever known it before.

The nightly visits to my room and my game of bed-hopping continued. I would wrap myself in extra blankets hoping he wouldn't unwrap me. But that was only hope. I definitely couldn't tell my mom during her visits because he had so enthralled her. I didn't know the word then like I know it today, but he was *grooming* and enticing her in order to keep me quiet.

The next step in controlling me was to no longer allow my boyfriend on my uncle's property. Then the prom that I had so dreamed of attending was no longer mine to attend. I was trapped. I was going to burst at any moment. I was going to survive or die, but either way I needed to escape. I tried again to end my life by taking a lot of

Tylenol. I didn't know that I wanted to really die. I just knew I wanted all of it to stop. I took enough to make me sick and fall asleep but not enough to sleep forever. I woke up to him in my room, holding the bottle and asking, "What did you do?" I was caught again with no end in the near future.

One afternoon my uncle came into my room. It was my breaking point, and I started fighting him off. I think maybe it made a difference that it wasn't dark because it was the darkness that made me scared. But for some reason the daylight gave me hope. I decided it was the day that I was going to go after him. It wasn't a calculated decision, but at that very moment I knew he was never again going to come to me in the darkness. No longer were his gross fingers going to touch me again. No longer was his body going to bury me and mine be taken over by him.

I turned into a madwoman. I remember that day vaguely because I think it was like an out-of-body experience. I just kept screaming and kicking. I was enraged and nothing was going to stop me. He locked me in my room, and I fell asleep in complete exhaustion. I woke up the next morning ready to go to school. I walked into that school and marched right to that nurse's office. I introduced myself and told them what had been happening to me. I told them of the nights. I told them everything.

5

That was the last day that I would ever have to sleep over there again. I remember somebody taking me to the house to get my stuff. Once again, I was throwing everything into a garbage bag as if I was an orphan with no place to go. But this time being an orphan didn't feel so bad because I was free. I put Josephine on top of all my belongings. I packed her last so she would be the first thing that I would see when I got to wherever I was going. I didn't have to tell her my secret anymore because this time it had been happening in the very place she lived with me. There were more tear stains on her than ever before. But we were free!

Being put in a car with somebody that I did not know and driving to a place with no idea where it was or who lived there brought fear and apprehension but also gave me a sense of freedom. Maybe this time somebody would really care for me. Maybe this time I would really be safe and wouldn't be hurt anymore.

We pulled into a driveway on a road called Clark Street, and the family's last name was Clark. I thought it was kind of funny and wondered if they had bought the street that they lived on. Maybe this family was rich because all the neighbors paid them something to live on their street? What did I know as a 16-year-old girl?

We got out of the car, walked up to the door and knocked, and this older woman answered. I was a little nervous because I had never been in a house with somebody that I did not know. I didn't know how to act, where to put my hands, or what to say. I was a little scared because I wasn't sure what was going to happen or what was even happening at that moment.

I don't remember much except that I had a bunk bed, which at first gave me a little bit of fear. But there was another girl living in my room, so I didn't think anything bad would happen to me. I remember the parents sitting me down at the kitchen table and explaining that we had chores to do but also would have freedoms. As long as I kept up my responsibilities, I could go places like to school basketball games, the mall, or the movies.

I had a case worker who was the one that had arranged my going into foster care. She took me to a court hearing about my accusations of my uncle. I was to tell my story of what happened in the darkest of night at my uncle's house and about how he made days dark too. So much of that day is all muddled together, but the thing I remember clearest is my mom walking into the court room holding hands with my uncle.

I've never been shot before, so I'm not sure, but the feeling that I had felt like a gun bullet going into my gut. I think that if I ever did get shot, that's what it would've felt like. I was devastated, numb, and lost for words. I had never felt truly loved by my mom, but that was the ultimate betrayal. That was the ultimate test and proof of the hate I felt she had for me.

I remember being asked questions and told that I had to tell my story. Then I was cross-examined… by my uncle. You would think, since it was a sexual abuse and assault case, that the perpetrator wouldn't have been allowed to be his own defense counsel. But this was 35 years ago, before the #metoo movement. This was before victims had a voice, before we talked about the dirty secrets that happened within the four walls of somebody's home. This was before we didn't think it was cute that dirty old men had little girls sitting on their laps. This was before a child had a voice. So I guess it shouldn't have surprised me when he stood up and started asking me questions.

I really thought the judge would've said that this was uncalled for or maybe the social worker that was there to protect me would've put a stop to it. But nobody did. I sat on that stand and had to raise my right hand to "tell the truth and nothing but the truth, so help me God." That dirty old man stared me in the eyes and asked me questions about what I did in back seats of cars. I had to listen to him ask me questions about the clothing that I wore, if I was a flirt, and if I liked men's attentions.

A lot of that day has blurred and stained the back of my mind forever. It burned within my soul as a day I felt forgotten. When he was all done cross-examining me and everything was said that needed to be said, the judge gave his verdict. My uncle had to stay at least a hundred yards away from me for eighteen months. He could not be anywhere near me and could not speak or even gesture to me. It didn't really matter to me what his sentence was because I didn't think that I would ever see him again. The pain and the trauma was already part of my life. I would never get those days back.

There have always been rumors of an underlying relationship between my uncle and mother. I was told there were many arguments about me, but nobody really knows for certain the exact details. I remember times when there were secrets and whispers when I walked into a room. I still don't know whether or not to believe some of the rumors. One thing that was certain that day in court was that going home was not an option. My mother was found to be unfit, somebody that couldn't take me back. The woman that was supposed to be my protector, someone that I was supposed to know really loved me, walked out of the courtroom the same way she walked… with him. I couldn't wait to get back to my doll.

Many people talk about foster homes and how there are some that only do it for the money, where children suffer worse within the walls of the foster home than even what they have experienced in their own home. But that's not what it was like here. It was safe and felt like family. There were real conversations, dinner table talk, a chore chart and schedules that we had choices with. This was all something I had never experienced. They gave side hugs and didn't get into my space. They had boundaries, made me feel human and that I had a voice.

Wanting to teach me responsibility, they got me a summer job at a Girl Scout camp. I worked in the kitchen washing dishes and stayed in a cabin with other girls that also worked in the kitchen. It was one of the best times I've ever had. I'm not sure how to explain it, but I felt important. I really felt like they were setting me up for success.

But I ruined it…

A bunch of girls and I snuck out of the camp, went to a dance hall, and brought some people back to the cabin to dance the night away. If I could go back to that moment I would do things so much different. It cost me my job, and I knew that I had really disappointed my *family*. I called them family because they really felt like it, and I really let them down.

They picked me up from camp and took me to their summer home on Keuka Lake. My foster sister and I slept outside in a tent, swam all day in the lake, and laid out in the sun. Tanning was extremely important in those days. We used lemon juice in our hair and baby oil on our skin.

We met some people on a boat, and they talked us into coming down to the lake in the evening for a party. My foster sister was more courageous and adventurous than I was. She talked me into sneaking out of our tent and running down to the party boat… another decision that I wish I hadn't made! If we got caught I knew the disappointment would be too great and they would ask me to leave. I knew that I was probably going to be blamed as a culprit. But at that moment we were sixteen years old, wanting an adventure and never looking to the consequences. We snuck out twice that week, and the second time we got caught.

I got scared my foster family would ask me to leave because I was "bad." Instead of facing the consequences and disappointment in their eyes, I ran away! I took what stuff I had from camp and walked and walked. I cried most of the time that I was walking. For the first time I felt like I was the one at fault, and that wasn't a good feeling. I never wanted to hurt this family because they truly gave me a home. And now I found myself walking the streets of Bath, New York wondering "Where am I to go?"

I needed to cry and stain Josephine's face even more with my tears. I needed to hide with her in a dark closet so nobody could see me cry. Walking down the road with just my small bag of clothes brought me to tears. I wished I could go back to my foster home because it was one of the first places in a very long time that I felt loved. They didn't have to love me or treat me as if I was theirs. But I had ruined it and, instead of dealing with the consequences, chose to run. I didn't choose to run because I couldn't handle the consequences. I chose to run because I couldn't look them in the face and know that I had disappointed them. They were so kind to me, and yet I failed them.

It was really hot as I walked the 17 miles from Keuka Lake to Bath, New York. I had no idea where I was going or how I was going to get there because I hadn't thought any of that through, but I didn't except any rides. I just kept walking. Leaving my new family was the last thing I wanted to do, but now I felt like I couldn't go back. I didn't know what it was to humble myself or that if I just told them I was sorry that they would still love me and take me in. My whole life until then had been based on conditions, never having felt unconditional love except from my grandmother and of course my rag doll.

When I got to Bath, the town was having a fair. I went to the store, bought a set of new clothes, and walked around the fairgrounds. Still having no idea what I was going to do, and not really caring at that moment, I walked around playing games, watching people and riding the rides. But as it got dark I had to find a solution. I had to come up with a plan.

Regretting it but seeing no other option, I ended up calling my mom. I told her where I was and that I needed a ride. She actually came to get me. I will never forget the moment when I saw my uncle pull up in his car, my mother pull up next to him, and they traded vehicles. I could not believe she brought my uncle or that she was driving me home in his car. You can only imagine my disbelief and rage! I was so angry but yet on the verge of crying because it felt like I now definitely knew the truth, that it was him and her against me.

We drove in complete silence. When we got to the house, I walked upstairs to my old bedroom and fell asleep. I woke up the next morning and knew I wasn't staying there. There was no way I was going to stay within those four walls, trapped in that house again… not after I had experienced a taste of love and boundaries. I had to come up with a solution, had to find a way out of there. So I got dressed and walked to town.

When I got there I saw a guy that I thought was really cute a while back. He worked at the five-and-dime store in our little town and was standing outside as I walked by. He flirted a little, and I flirted back. When he asked me where I was staying I told him I had just gotten back and was staying at my mom's but that there was no way I was going to stay one more night there. He told me if I wanted to I could stay at his apartment. I found out that one of my friends from high school was living there too with her boyfriend so I didn't feel like I would be totally alone. I would be with friends.

But it was such an awkward situation. He had a girlfriend, but I had no place to go. I still had some money from working at the Girl Scout camp, so I was able to buy some groceries and other things I needed. The situation was made more awkward because I wasn't allowed to be there during the day and then there was a lot of partying, drinking, and drugs every night. I tried to stay away from it for the most part, but like most teenagers, bad choices often clouded my decisions.

I tried to find someplace else to live, to lay my head to sleep at night, but refused to go back home. I really wanted to just go back to my foster home and tell them how sorry I was, but something, probably my pride, wouldn't allow me to do that. I knew that the situation that I had put myself in now wasn't going to end well, and I ended up having a physical relationship with this guy.

I found a job working at McDonald's. It gave me money and a sense of purpose. It was someplace to go instead of wandering the streets. Those days are pretty foggy because there was so much going on in that apartment.

My sister came over a few times, and they always wanted to play truth and dare. It was a game that I was not interested in because I knew they were hoping for dares, like having us walk out in lingerie, and I was not a willing to do that. My seventeen-year-old sister was manipulated into giving my "boyfriend", who was ten years older, sexual favors. I found out when I walked in on them one day. I just stood there watching for a few moments before, in disbelief of what my eyes were seeing, I walked out of the apartment in disbelief.

I hadn't lived there very long before I had had enough… enough of the drug deals, the parties and of being a secret because he also had a much older "day girlfriend." I had enough of feeling not enough and not being loved. I felt myself spiraling out of control, not from drugs and alcohol but from emotions and lack of self-worth. I needed to find a way out. Once again I found myself trying to find a way to end this terrible life that I was living.

I could feel my mind playing with me. If I was standing in the mirror I felt like my mind would pop out at me and tell me how unworthy I was. My mind would tell me how ugly I was and that how I was that day wasn't going to change in ten years. What I was doing and who I was was all life was ever going to offer me as a second-class girl. I felt distorted when I looked at myself, having no idea how to pick myself back up and realize that I could make a choice to get out of all of this. The only choice that kept popping in my head was death. I felt that if I died nobody would care or look for me, much less cry. I felt abandoned, all alone, and didn't know how to get my worth back.

6

One evening in late December 1986, not long after finding my boyfriend with my sister, I walked across the street from his apartment to the police station. I walked into the office of an officer that I knew and sat down. He asked, "Bambi, what are you doing here?" I responded, "I don't know. I don't feel right, and I feel lost." He asked if I needed help and I again said, "I don't know." He inquired further by asking if my boyfriend had done something to me, and I responded, "No, I just walked out."

Then I just got up, left his office, and walked out of the station and down to the bridge in our town. I got up on top of the bridge and looked down into the water. In that moment, I felt peaceful as I looked at the water, like it could and was willing to take me. It felt like my solution as I contemplated if I would lose anything in my life if I just ended it. How long would it take for somebody to even find me? And would anybody even know or care that I was missing?

At that very moment I decided my life wasn't worth living anymore and I was going to jump. As I was ready to say goodbye to myself, I felt somebody reach for me, pull me back, and throw me to the ground. I remember kicking and screaming and saying, "Please let me go!" It was the officer whose office I had just walked out of who was restraining me. He put me in the back of his police car and drove me back to the police station.

I was crying because I had failed. The hopelessness had so overtaken me that I couldn't even breathe. Someone from where I had been staying across the street saw me in the cop car, and soon there were several people standing next to it. The officer began asking them questions. He asked my boyfriend specifically if he had done something to me. "I swear to God, no!" he responded. The officer asked everyone if I was on drugs, and they all said that I wasn't taking anything but had just walked out of the house as if I knew where I was going, as if I had a purpose that I didn't share with them.

The officer got back in the car with me and drove away. In that moment I knew even more what it felt to be totally alone because there was no rag doll with me. There was nobody to tell this deep secret to, nobody to understand what I was going through. My rag doll Josephine couldn't be there. For the first time I was walking this journey all alone and didn't know whether I wanted to survive it.

I couldn't imagine where he was taking me! All I knew is that I was in the back seat of a police car and we were going down the road. I was really so numb and lost that I didn't even care if he dumped me on the side of the road. We pulled up to a big building that looked like a hospital, and I was taken in. No one told me it was the Buffalo Psychiatric Center. They took me into a room that had a bed and a chair. The room was green and had no pictures or decorations hanging on the wall. The door had a glass window and more windows on the one wall to see outside of the room into the hallway. People were sitting out there and smoking. I remember watching a girl go up and down the hall in her hospital gown, talking to herself and saying that she knew John F. Kennedy. I had no idea where I was or what was going to happen to me. All I knew was that I was in a strange place and I couldn't open the door to get out.

A doctor came in and began to ask me questions. One of the questions was how old I was, and I told him I was sixteen. He left the room for a moment and came back and said that I was too young to be at that facility and that they were going to take me someplace else for children my age. I still was in a fog and didn't understand what that meant. They just kept asking me how I felt and if I still had suicidal thoughts. My reply was, "Can you give me some ideas what to live for? Can you tell me something that's worth living for?"

I don't know whether he liked my comment, but he wrote it down on a piece of paper, put it inside a folder, told me to wait there, and left the room. A few hours later I was transported by ambulance to another facility. This one didn't look like a hospital, but there were a lot of buildings around. I saw a sign but don't remember what the sign said.

When I got into the building I realized I was at a psychiatric center for kids. It kind of looked like a school classroom. I was taken to another office that was covered with glass windows so you could see outside into the halls. There was a young kid sitting and watching TV and another kid sitting at a table writing things on a piece of paper.

They put me in an exam room, took some blood work, and asked me if I had any clothes. I looked down at what I was wearing and was totally shocked that my clothes did not match. I had pajamas on and pants with bold colors and a lot of designs on them. I was a little mortified of what I looked like because I always tried really hard to match and look my best. But at the same time, at this moment, there was part of me that just didn't care.

They continued to ask me questions. Some questions I didn't know the answer to and some I didn't even care about.

As they examined me, they asked if I had any bruises, bites, blade marks or birthmarks. And they kept writing down everything.

After I was done with the examination they gave me some clothes from a closet and showed me to another room. In the room there were four beds with towels, blankets, and sheets on one of them. I was told to make my bed and get situated. I was coming around and didn't know why I was there, so I asked a nurse. I was told that they were concerned about my thought process of wanting to end my life. She said I wasn't allowed to stay in the room after getting settled. When she left, the door shut and I could hear the click of the lock that kept people from entering without a key.

After making my bed, I walked out to where there were other people sitting and just sat there wondering what I was supposed to do next. The rest of the day was kind of a blur. I went to bed and the next morning was told to go into the office. When I went in, I was asked to sit down. There was a doctor there with a folder. He opened up the folder, looked over my paperwork, and asked if I knew that I was pregnant.

I don't know what the look on my face was, but I know what the feeling inside was. I felt a gurgling in my stomach, anxiousness, fear, and disbelief. I couldn't comprehend the words "you are pregnant" in my mind. I was off balance and think if I was standing I would've fallen to the ground and passed out.

I was told that I would have to go to the doctor to be examined and should think about terminating the pregnancy. They said that, due to the state I was in, it probably would not be a good idea to bring a child into the world when I wanted to end my world. I knew at that moment that I wouldn't let that happen but didn't know what my next steps were going to be or what the next moment was going to hold. They made arrangements for me to see a doctor and be put on some vitamin pills until I could be taken to my doctor's appointment.

I needed to be alone and asked to go back to my room. They said we weren't allowed to do such a thing normally, as we needed to always be supervised, but that they would let me go long enough to compose myself. I got up, opened the door, and walked down the hall. A nurse let me into my room and I fell to the floor and cried.

There were so many thoughts running through my head. At first I was so scared and thought, "How could this have happened?" I was rattled that there was a life inside of me and I had tried to jump off a bridge to end mine. In hindsight, what took me to the brink of unpremeditated suicide could have been pregnancy hormones mixed with a lifelong sense of unworthiness. In the moment, all that was certain was that I was in shock. What were people going to say? How was I going to explain how this happened?

I thought about who the father was. I couldn't imagine being with him for the rest of my life and living his kind of lifestyle. I thought of the pending embarrassment, the bullying, and how people would stare at me. How was I going to tell my mom? How do girls like me have babies?

I remember touching my stomach then and realizing that there was life inside. I cried again. This little being growing inside of me was going to be a person that I was responsible for. I laid on the floor and just kept crying because I didn't know what else to do. I was all by myself. This was big news in my life, but I had nobody to share it with. I had nobody to tell the secret to. My rag doll was sitting in a garbage bag somewhere. She wasn't there to have my tears stain her face.

I remember looking up to Heaven. I always looked at God as a dad with a baseball bat, ready to clock me on the head if I did anything wrong. Here I was in a psychiatric center for teenagers, lying on the floor because I just heard the news that I was pregnant. I could only imagine that that clock on my head was going to happen pretty soon. But when I looked up to Heaven, I said, "If there is really a God, would You have some kind of mercy on me and show me the way? If You have any kind of kindness in Your heart, would You help me?"

I prayed that somehow, someway I would honor and surrender my life to Him if He would just make sure my baby was safe and provide a way for me to take care of it! I kept looking up to Heaven waiting for God's response. The heavens didn't miraculously open, nor did I feel like I got a hit on my head, but I did feel a sense of peace. For the first time ever I felt the love of a God that I had thought only punishes. For the first time in my life I felt that I was going to be taken care of. Somehow this little life inside of me had given *me* life. At that moment I didn't need Josephine Priscilla, my rag doll, because I had a sense that I now had God. I remember getting up with a smile on my face thinking, "I am going to be a mommy, and everything is going to be okay."

I spent twenty-eight days and turned seventeen in that place. It was another birthday that would have felt insignificant except for the fact that I had a life inside of me. That made it one of the greatest birthdays. There was a sense of peace because God and I had a conversation and I knew he was going to take care of me. God continued to show me how much he had my back as there was no appointment being made for the termination of the life that was growing inside of me.

Someone made a call to the psychiatric center stating that they were willing to take me into their home. To my surprise it was a pastor and his family whose church I had gone to one time and where I must've filled out a visitor's card. The pastor had also been a softball referee one year when I was forced to play softball. I didn't know what to think. There were so many thoughts and questions running through my mind. Why did they want me? They didn't know me, and I really didn't know them. How would they ever want a stranger, much less a pregnant one, and eventually a teen mom and baby living in their house? What was going to be the cost of living there? But all I kept thinking was that God was walking through this with me and He was taking care of the details.

I can't tell you how I felt when I walked out of those psychiatric center doors. But I can tell you that the thought of ending my life was no longer part of my inner dialogue. The only dialogue I had now was how I was going to make sure that this baby, this life that was living inside of me, was going to have the best life possible. I settled in to life in my new surroundings. I had a bedroom that I fixed up, making it my own. I got my job back at McDonald's and started just living life again.

It wasn't always easy. At times I was bullied by people because they found out who the father was. He would come into my job and tell me we could get married. I told him that there was absolutely no way, that I didn't want anything to do with him and that I would make sure that he would never have anything to do with me or my baby.

I began buying things for the arrival of my new precious gift. When I made a blanket, bought a crib and decorated inside of it, the first thing that went inside was my rag doll Josephine Priscilla. She had protected me all of these years, and now it was going to be her turn to protect this precious little baby who was going to sleep in this bedroom.

I had to go to my mom's house to tell her that I was pregnant. I planned a time that I knew she was probably going to be getting ready for work or something. When I got there my mother was in the bathtub. I sat on the toilet seat and told her that I was going to be a mom. I don't know why I felt the need to tell her since I wasn't living with her and didn't feel like she supported or was there for me at all. I guess I did it out of respect because, even though I didn't feel loved by her, she still was my mom.

She was shocked and asked me what I was going to do about taking care of the baby. She made it clear that she wasn't going to support me and that I had to figure it out myself. I didn't say anything in response. Her words didn't really affect me because I already knew that she wasn't going to help me, and I didn't want her help. I knew she wasn't that kind of mom.

There actually was a glimpse at a moment around the end of my pregnancy when I felt like I was important to her. First, she took me to the mall and bought an elephant stuffed animal, really pretty pajamas, and a housecoat for me to take to the hospital. I felt a little connected to her for the first time. Then the family I was living with had a vacation planned close to my due date, so I stayed at her house and went into labor there.

I knew without a shadow of a doubt when I went into labor. It was one of the most painful things I had experienced but led to the most joyful thing that I had ever held in my arms… my beautiful daughter! I can't even put into words the feelings and love that I had for that precious little girl. I held her so tight and knew that she was a gift. No matter what happened in my life, she would bring me so much joy and had been used by God to bring me to Him.

She was so beautiful and tiny. I couldn't comprehend all the love that I felt for her. Now I had a responsibility to always hold her close. At that moment I felt like I would never need my rag doll again to tell my secrets to because now I could tell them to my beautiful daughter. Life was perfect, and it seemed like there would never be any darkness again.

I continued to stay at my mom's for the first few days after being released from the hospital, and she was really kind. I didn't quite know how to react to that but really didn't care because no matter what happened now I was going to be a mom and she wasn't going to be able to hurt me (or my baby) like she had in the past ever again. I am now grateful for those special moments that we shared together. I felt like she looked at me differently than ever before.

When the pastor's family came home, my baby girl and I went back there. I could never have imagined what it was like to be a mom! There were long nights of bottle-feeding and constant crying. I looked at my beautiful daughter as a miracle but wondered if I was really going to be a good mom to her. Being up all night with her and then having to work in the mornings left me in tears too. I didn't understanding why, if God had given me this beautiful miracle, I couldn't get it together.

I had to learn what all these cries meant. Was she hungry? Was she wet? Did she just want to be held? Was she sick? Or was she just trying to find her voice? We got into a routine. I would get up in the morning, take her to day care, and walk to work. After working my eight hours, I'd pick her up, come back home, and hold her. We would play and experience all of her firsts together

7

One day at work, as I was stationed in the drive-through, a man ordered a Big Mac, large fry, and Coke. I didn't think anything of his order until he came to the window. I realized it was a guy that I briefly had a childhood crush on from the church that I had attended my whole life. I looked at him, he looked at me, and we both had a shocked look on our faces. I was just in disbelief and didn't know what to say.

He was what I considered a true "church kid." His family was popular there, and his mother played the organ. Here was every church girl's dreamboat looking at me in my drive-through window, asking me questions about my life. At first I really didn't even think he knew who I was. We had had such a brief crush on each other back when I was thirteen. I still had a couple of letters that he had written to me during those brief months telling me I was a real fox but to make sure I didn't tell anybody that he wrote to me.

We had a back-and-forth conversation on what we were doing with our lives. He was working on a farm, and I told him bluntly that I was taking care of my baby and working at McDonald's. He asked if he could call me. I told him to look my phone number up in the phone book. I never imagined that he would actually call me that evening.

As he drove away I had butterflies fluttering. However, I had no intention of getting involved with anybody because I just wanted to be a good mom. I wanted to make sure that my daughter had a chance in this world and knew how much I loved her. She would never need a rag doll named Josephine Priscilla to tell her secrets to because I would be the kind of mom that she could speak into my ear and I would trust, believe, and comfort her.

But that evening the telephone rang! We talked for hours about everything that had gone on in our lives so far, what we were doing now, and what our future plans looked like. I got off the phone and told the people that I was living with that I just met the man I was going to marry! I was as sure as the sun went up every morning that that was the man that I would spend the rest of my life with. I had no doubt that those fluttering feelings that were happening inside of my body were real and that one day I would be his wife!

The next day he came to my house and picked me up for my very first real date. He was such a gentleman. He opened up the car door for me and closed it when I got in. We had an amazing conversation. He drove me to Batavia, New York, and we went to dinner at a Perkins. I still remember that we sat in the second booth as you walked in. I made him order my dinner because I had only been to one other restaurant in my life. The funny thing is that other time had been with his grandparents when I had won a Sunday school contest years ago.

I had rib eye steak and carrots, but I didn't like carrots so, I kind of swirled them around my plate so he wouldn't know that I didn't care for carrots. We continued to talk so easily and laughed a lot. I became even more convinced that this was my future husband. We had a whirlwind of a romance! Back in those days there were no cell phones. I would hide myself in the hall every evening, talking the night away on the home phone.

He said he wanted to take me to where he worked. I tried looking cute by dressing up in white shorts and sandals. It didn't register in my brain that he was a farmer and milked cows. We pulled up to a barn. I wanted to impress him so I got out as if it was no big deal. I fed my first calf that day and had to put my fingers in his mouth so it would start him sucking on the bottle. It was one of the grossest things I'd ever had to do in my seventeen years of life. But I wanted to impress my future husband.

He worked a lot of hours, always exhausted because he milked in the morning, cleared hay or wheat fields, and then would have to milk again. We were in love and it was a fast love. I could not get enough of his presence and just always wanted to be with him. When I wasn't able to, it did produce some insecurity. I was still a hurt little girl with so many trust and abandonment issues. I didn't know that's what they were called at that time, but I know now that I'm older.

He asked me to marry him with a cute little ring that had diamonds and rubies in it. I just knew he was the one and never second-guessed or looked back. Of course I would marry him. There were no questions but only the answer, "Yes I will be your wife." All I knew or cared was that I was marrying a man who was raised in a two-parent household, attended church, and had family members that were in the ministry. He had gone to a Christian school and college. I knew that he was a hard worker and would be a good provider.

I was excited to be engaged to somebody that had lived all the things that I dreamed about as a little girl. My daughter was going to have a good life. She was going to have a family with two parents and church on Sunday and extended family that doted over her. We prepared for a wedding in May. The pastor whose family I was living with was going to marry us. We were getting everything all set up and organized.

I was told that his parents were not thrilled but didn't understand why. I was informed that they thought it was too fast and, besides that, I was not a virgin and was bringing someone else's child into the marriage. They didn't see my heart, a heart that just wanted to serve Jesus. They were only able to see this teen mom with a baby girl and their son having to take on the responsibility of being a dad when he was so young himself. But we continued to march forward, planning for a wedding and forever lifetime together.

A month before the wedding he sat me down on the couch. He was fumbling around with his hands, and I kept asking what was going on. He told me that he wasn't ready to get married and wanted to end the relationship with me. I was shocked, stunned, devastated, and hurt. I had so many questions and no answers. There were so many things running through my head, and nothing stopped the circles going around and around and around. I cried uncontrollably. I didn't understand. He told me that he did not want me to contact him and that we would have no other conversations with each other. This was the best way for him. I asked him if he found somebody else and he told me he had!!

At that very moment I felt second-class once again. I felt like a secret again. I felt unwanted again. The devastation of my broken heart was unbearable to pick up and put back together again. I didn't know how to control my emotions as they spiraled out of control but didn't think about ending my life. I needed to run to my little girl as well as my rag doll and have this pain go away. When he left I picked up my daughter, searched for my doll, lay on my bed, and just wept!

What could I have done differently? What was wrong with me that nobody wanted to love me? "Why?" was the only question that I could ask God. I had promised Him that day in the room at the psychiatric center that I would serve Him. I didn't understand the journey that I was on or the test I was going through. I didn't know what it was going to cost to serve Him or what that really meant and at that moment couldn't even think about it. I just cried and let the tears fall onto my rag doll once again.

I walked around in a daze! I didn't even notice if I was breathing because my heart was so broken. I tried to go on with my days and weeks, but nothing could take away the pain. I couldn't put the pieces back together of my broken heart. For the first time ever, I was lovesick. I really didn't understand what that meant at the time but knew that my heart hurt so badly, and my mind couldn't comprehend any of the pain.

It was the first time I realized that, no matter how much pain I was in, I was still a mom and had responsibilities. I had to go on, as I no longer had only me to take care of. I think being a mom helped my mind to not contemplate thinking of ending the pain, of going back to that bridge and jumping. I needed to keep getting up and survive for my little girl. I couldn't fall into a deep dark hole. If I did, who would take care of her? Having her feel like her mom had failed her was something I never wanted to become a reality.

After a few weeks went by, I received a phone call from my ex-fiancé asking if I wanted to go with him for ice cream. I was a little shocked but also relieved that maybe he really did still love me. Maybe it wasn't a fairy tale that had come to an end. I remember him picking me up, as I didn't drive yet or have a car. So he came to the house, and then we drove to the ice cream shop in town. I cried a little but also tried holding my emotions back so he could talk and tell me what happened. I wanted to know what I had done that was wrong. How could he love me one minute and not want to be with me the next? I needed to know.

He told me he had missed me and that he was sorry for how much he hurt me. He wanted to date again but take it slow, not thinking of marriage right then. He said he loved me and just didn't realize how much until he walked away. I asked about the other girl. He told me it was over, that she was too young.

I was jumping up and down inside, my body feeling like it was going to come out of itself because I wasn't rejected. In hindsight, I wish that at that very moment I could've been older and had a talk with that younger me. I would have told her to run, but I don't think it would've worked because my heart was already his, and there is no way of getting around that. I wanted to be his wife. I wanted to walk into church together. I wanted my life to intertwine with his and for it to never unravel again.

We decided that we would date and take it slow. But when love overtakes your mind and you have already experienced the things we had with each other, that love just takes you. You're on a race track, inside of a fast car, driving as fast as you possibly can around the track.

There's no thought of stopping or escape. And so he changed his mind, deciding he wanted to be married before his birthday. I asked when his birthday was just out of shock, knowing that it was not far off. We ended up choosing a date just three weeks after that day at the ice cream parlor when we had decided to take it slow.

He told me he didn't want a big wedding. I was saddened that there would be no white dress or flowers, no pretty invitations that would I send, and no parties to celebrate me or getting married. Although I was disappointed, I also just wanted to marry this man that every girl from our youth group had wanted. I had won the prize of our church. He picked me!!

We had premarital counseling with the pastor, but I really don't think we even listened. We knew we would get married regardless, so nothing that was said really mattered. Our wedding day was one of the hottest of that summer, and it felt like an oven where I was getting ready in my upstairs apartment. Even though the day wasn't anything like what I had dreamt up as a little girl of what a wedding day was supposed to look or feel like, at least I was marrying the man of my dreams. He was someone that I couldn't wait to spend the rest of my life with.

Our guests were my mom, his parents, our youth group leaders, and the family that was going to my daughter for the weekend. There were people at the church cleaning, and they came in to watch us get married too. It was a very fast wedding, not lasting more than 20 minutes. But I was married. I had officially won the heart of this man. His parents were not happy, but what were they going to do? We were young, foolish, and thought we had all the answers.

My mom had a little get-together at her house. We had angel food cake and all sat around in her living room. A couple people gave us gifts of boxed fans, perfect for how hot that day was. We were dripping with sweat. Nobody stayed around very long, and we just wanted to get to Niagara Falls to start our honeymoon.

We felt so proud to be a newly married couple. We had grabbed life by the bull horns and were going to conquer the world. As we drove away from my mom's house, I remembered the three letters he had written to me as a young 13-year-old girl, saying that I was his fox, someday we would get married, have two little girls, and to please not tell anyone that he wrote me the letters. It gave me a little bit of a chuckle as I thought, "One girl, and one to go..."

Our honeymoon was brief because it was planting season, and my husband was the only workhand for the family farm he worked for. We had a good time walking the main road and having our picture taken and put on a magazine that said "Honeymooners." But the weather was still very hot, and we were mostly looking forward to just starting our life. I also really missed my daughter, as it was the first time I was away from her. Even though I knew she was being taken care of and the other kids where she was staying were just doting on her, I still wanted her in my arms again.

The day we were leaving Niagara Falls, as we were driving out of the hotel parking lot, we had to stop to let people cross the street. I absolutely could not believe my eyes. The very first man that I had slept with was pushing a stroller, walking across the street with his wife and two children. We locked eyes when we saw each other, each knowing without a shadow of a doubt who the other was.

I remember being so caught off guard that I jerked my head back in complete shock. As I was sitting there next to my new husband, the person that I was going to spend the rest of my life with, I felt shame pass over me. There was so much guilt, as if I had somehow betrayed him by having already sold my love, all for a moment's hope for a relationship that would never come to pass.

My husband looked at me, and I looked at him. He asked the question that I was hoping he wouldn't. "Who is that?" I could have lied and he would've never known. I could have washed over the question, pretending that the man just looked like somebody I knew. But I didn't want to start this life, with the man that I wanted to be with forever, with a lie.

I told him that was the man I had such a crush on when I was younger, who I snuck out of the house in the middle of the night to drink wine with, and that I lay on his couch and gave away my virginity. That was the man that had taken what I should've given to this man next to me in the driver's seat of our car. That moment of shame had continued to haunt me whenever I heard stories about women that gave away their virginity. There were stories told during Bible studies and teen groups, which taught that whoever you had been with is who you were bringing into your marriage.

I sat in that car feeling so ashamed, but at that moment my husband reached over, touched my leg, and told me it was going to be okay. It was *our* life that was starting. His reassurance didn't take away my feeling of wanting to pull over on the side of the road and just vomit it all up. I just wanted to wash that moment out of my mind, but it was ingrained and would never leave.

8

After coming back from our honeymoon at Niagara Falls, he moved all of his stuff to my little one-bedroom studio apartment and, we began life. When you marry a farmer, his life is the field. It is barn chores and cows that don't milk themselves. He worked a lot of hours. Because my apartment was far from his job, he didn't get home until really late at night. We needed to move closer to where he worked.

We began looking and found a little two-bedroom apartment up near the train tracks in Warsaw, New York. Everything that happened in the apartments around us could be heard through the walls. The train would come by often and shake the apartment. But I was happy! I was so happy to be his wife.

I didn't have an example in my own life of what it meant to be a wife but wanted to do it just right. I knew I needed to cook and clean, make the house presentable for him, and be available any time that he needed me. I craved his attention and desired his touch. Everything to do with him was perfect to me, and if anything became a problem between us, I assumed I was the one with all the issues. Nothing could ever be his fault.

I thought that if you married a man from the church, somebody whose parents had been Christians forever, and that if you go to church, that things were always supposed to work out. I couldn't figure out why he was always mad at me, why he was always tired and didn't want to be near me. I couldn't figure out why love didn't feel the way that I thought it was going to.

Soon after we were married I started feeling tired and sick all the time, with no motivation. I was pregnant. I thought he would've been thrilled, excited that we were going to have a child together. My daughter was going to have a sibling. But when I told him, his face froze with no emotion that I could read. He got into his car and took off for work.

I was numb. I just told my husband, the man that I was going to spend the rest of my life with, that our family was growing. Yet his response was no different than the response others had given last time when I wasn't married and told people that I was pregnant. I really thought it would be different when you got married. Maybe I had watched too much TV and read too many romantic stories. He came home that evening and told me he was sorry for how he reacted. He was just caught off guard.

We continued to live our life and tried to grow in unity with each other. We moved from our little apartment by the railroad tracks and got a cute little half house down the road. My belly grew, and we began preparing for the arrival of our new little baby. When I had my beautiful second daughter we were happy! He was full of joy! It was one of the most magical moments in my life as we both held our new baby girl. Things couldn't have been better. There were so many dreams and plans for the next part of our life. He participated at home, holding her all the time and changing diapers.

We were intimate soon after I had our daughter, never thinking anything of it. That was until I went to the doctor's again and realized I was pregnant with my third child. You could only imagine the fear that I had going home to tell my husband. His response wasn't as dramatic as when I told him the first time, but it wasn't happiness and he wasn't joyous. He was quiet. I wished I knew what was running through his head. I wished I knew his thoughts.

One morning I woke up and everything became clear when I read a letter that said, "I am not coming home. I don't want to be married. I don't want this life." I was shocked and devastated. Now I was alone with two children and one on the way. What in the world was I going to do? What was wrong with me that I couldn't keep my husband happy? What was so terrible about me that I wasn't worth being loved? Why was my little girl outside walking the sidewalks calling for her daddy and asking the mailman, "Do you know where my daddy is?"

I did that! It was my fault that my daughter snuck out of the house to go find her daddy. If I could only understand what made him leave, then I could fix it. But all I could do was put my two daughters to bed and sit in the corner of the living room with my rag doll, rocking myself back and forth and crying until I fell asleep.

I woke up in the middle of the night on the floor. I couldn't have my daughter see me there. I couldn't have her see me cry. I couldn't have her see me staring into space and hear her asking her mommy what was wrong. I had to get it together! I had to figure it out. I couldn't cry in the corner with my rag doll anymore. I was a mom now and needed to get into action.

We only had one car, and I didn't know how to drive yet, so the girls and I were pretty much left alone. His family didn't like the idea that we got married, so they tried to convince him to stay away. We had been going to his uncle's church, and they checked up on me and said that they were praying. My life was pretty much the girls and I and my sorrow!

When you are such a broken child as I was, everything that happens to you continues to feed those thoughts of worthlessness in your mind. If I could just depend better, if I just wouldn't have said that, if I just didn't put uncooked kidney beans in the chili, if my bread just would've risen, if I just didn't get pregnant so fast, if I just wasn't so broken, then maybe he would've stayed.

He was gone a month. I found out he had gone to Virginia with a married woman but decided he wanted to come back. He was very apologetic and so sorry for what he put me through. We had to go to counseling with his uncle to try to figure out what was wrong.

At those sessions we found out that I came from a broken family and I didn't know what a good, healthy family looked like. I didn't know how to submit to the authority of my husband and needed to have women in the church teach me how to be a wife. If I'd learned those traits, then my husband wouldn't have wandering eyes or the desire to run.

So we fell back into the routine of being young parents and a young married couple trying to figure it out. I was on edge all the time. I was scared that I would do something wrong and that he would leave again. But in those early days I didn't have much time to think. I had a little toddler, a newborn baby, and another one on the way. I had to get my stuff together and figure this out. If I could just be a better girl, wife, mother, and person, then I wouldn't lose him again.

During the pregnancy with my third child we moved four different times. I would pack and unpack and pack again all of our belongings to settle our little family into a new place. Two of those times we had moved in with his grandmother and then his aunt and uncle. I was stressed and exhausted, but then a day in July we brought home our third little girl. My second daughter wasn't walking yet, and my oldest would be turning three in a month.

I became an extreme overachiever, wanting everything to be perfect. I decided the day that I got home from the hospital with my third child that I would harvest and can 30 quarts of beans for our family. My days were spent by myself with three little children as my husband worked long hours at the farm. Those days were like a blur, all blended together. I was just a young 20-year-old with three children under three, moving, keeping the house together, going to church, and trying with everything within me to be a good wife. Struggling with all the memories of the past that kept coming up, I kept trying to shove them back down. I was scared that I was going to blow one day and wouldn't be able to contain my emotions.

My husband took on another job in another area, which meant I had to pack up our belongings and move yet again. This time it was to a farmhouse in the country. I was excited because it was really big. But the former tenants were an older couple that had twenty-two cats and two dogs living in the house. They had left the house so dirty.

Moving in, I was cleaning and trying to get rid of the cats. But when I got rid of the cats, the mice came out. I would shop-vacuum up mice in my bathroom and living room. The bathroom looked like they hadn't cleaned it in all the years that they had lived there. With three little children underfoot all the time, I began cleaning room by room. I was in total exhaustion.

It was just before Thanksgiving, and we were going to have Thanksgiving in our house, so the perfectionist in me needed to make sure everything was perfect at any expense, even the expense of me being sick. I ended up in the hospital, finding out that I had caught salmonella from all the cat dander, feces, and filth that was in the house. I didn't have time to be sick. That wasn't part of the deal. I had to be a good wife and mom. I had to keep my husband's eyes only on me.

I did love that house and the space that we had. However, there were so many different problems that I had to learn to deal with myself because my husband worked long hours. I felt like we never saw him. He was always driving truck or in the field picking the harvest to take to the canning factory. Birds would fly in the house, and I would have to figure out how to get them out. The well would dry up, and I would have to carry water from the creek and boil it. One time the well dried up in the middle of canning peaches, and it was such a mess. We were away from everyone and didn't have much of a support system.

9

One evening when my husband got home from work, I had to tell him some news. I was so afraid. I couldn't wrap my head around the news myself and knew he wouldn't be able to either. I was scared that this was going to be another time he would leave and that this time he wouldn't come back. But I had to tell him. It's not like I could hide it for long. I was pregnant again with our fourth child. I had three children under three years old, now another one on the way, and was not even 22 years of age.

After I told him, I ran out to the car. I was planning to drive 100 miles per hour down the road, hoping I would hit a tree or something so I wouldn't have to deal with the rejection of him running and leaving me in the middle of the country with these children and pregnant again. But his reaction was so much better than I thought it was going to be. He ran out to the car in his underwear, telling me that things were going to be okay, that we were going to make it, and that he wasn't leaving. He wasn't blaming me. We were just going to be a family of six now.

But not everyone took the news well. His boss and wife were not happy. We were going to be without a job or place to live once again. During those few years my doll was nowhere to be found. I didn't have time to tell her my secrets. I didn't have time to rock her in a corner of a room. I had to be a big girl now and figure all of this out.

We found a house in Silver Springs, New York. The first two weeks, as we started settling in, we had a major flea problem. The prior occupants had dogs, and we did not. So the fleas had nowhere to go but to bite us continually. The house had to be flea bombed twice. That definitely was not the way I wanted to start building my new house into a home again.

I decided to start going to counseling to deal with the things of my past, to start walking through the steps of healing. I didn't know how much that journey was going to cost or how much pain I really carried within me. I didn't understand the effect that rejection had on me. At Bible studies, I was learning about who Jesus really was, and all I wanted was for Him to continue to fill my life. I would sit on the floor late at night crying out to Him to take away all of the pain. Exhausted from my tears and "why" questions, I would have to get up the next morning to be a mom to three little girls and the one that was growing inside of me. I wanted to be whole. I wanted to know what whole looked and felt like. I didn't realize then as much as I realize now that wholeness is a journey. It's one layer at a time.

One day I came home from taking my oldest daughter to dance lessons to a once again quiet house. My husband had run away again into the arms of another woman. He had been working two jobs, and one of the jobs happened to have been with the girl that he broke our engagement off for. I guess I hadn't understood the pull that she had on him.

I was devastated once again. I could not believe that he had walked out the door, now leaving me with four babies to take care of. I didn't understand how his relationship with her was more important than being a father, husband, and Christian man that served God. I didn't know then like I know now that his faith was never secure. He walked around with doubts of who God was all the time, but I still hung on to the truth that we were married for life and that God was going to work it out. I thought that somehow this had to be my fault. I never considered that I had carried the burden of moving my family ten times so far, had four babies in five years, and was overwhelmed with being a mom and trying really hard to be a good wife. I didn't realize the tremendous stress I was under.

The ladies of our church continued to encourage and help me again. We prayed all night that God would have mercy on me and bring back my husband. I promised that I would do better, be a better wife and mom, and submit more. I made all those promises to God because I never once thought that all of this couldn't have been my fault.

He decided to come back and ask for forgiveness. Once again we were in counseling with his uncle from the church that we went to. I heard that I needed to learn more about what a good wife was and to allow my husband to have the authority that he needed. If I would just get it together, he would stop leaving me for other women. I added that lie to the shame that I already carried from the past that I was trying to work through… the sexual and mental abuse, the physical hardship, and the lack of love that I had experienced.

Once again I started feeling like God was a god with a baseball bat and, if I didn't get it together, I was going to lose it all. My need for perfection came in like a roaring lion, fierce. I had to have everything perfect. I had to cook the perfect meals, be the perfect wife in our intimate times, and the perfect mom and homeschooling teacher. My children needed to perfectly stand at attention and be obedient because now I felt my life depended upon it. I didn't want God to renege on saving my soul! I never wanted Him to be disappointed in me like everybody else around me was. I carried so much guilt, and now even Josephine Priscilla couldn't help me. I was too ashamed to even look at her. My life was unraveling, my faith was being tested, and my past was knocking at my door and barging its way through.

Things began to get better between my husband and me. It seemed like he was humbled and back to being a husband and father. His focus seemed to be on being a family, searching the Word of God and finding his faith again. It seemed that life was going to get better and our love was going to continue to grow. We were getting into the groove and were going to make it a lifetime.

One hot summer afternoon, my husband was in the sandbox with our oldest daughter and I was in the house making homemade spaghetti sauce with my big pressure canner pot. I only had a long pajama shirt on, and my husband was outside with shorts and no shirt on. My pressure canner decided to seal. I called my husband into the house and asked him if he could unseal the pot because I wasn't using it for canning.

He came into the house, touched the button to take the steam out, and decided to lift up the top of the pot. As he did, the whole pot blew up. The scalding hot spaghetti sauce landed on both of us and my youngest little girl who was 18 months old. We immediately ran into the bathtub and turned on the cold water to stop the pain. The ambulance was called, and we were all rushed to the hospital.

Throughout the long ordeal we spent 17 days in a burn unit. Many times my husband was fighting for his life as his body had an infection. We had skin grafts done on our bodies. His was from his neck down to his chest. My breasts were skin grafted after seven days of scrubbing. It was the worst experience ever.

We were in separate rooms, and I felt helpless. I was dealing with my own pain, but my husband was in another room, many times fighting for his life. It was a long journey with so many emotions running through my head! It was me that decided to use a pressure cooker. It was me that called him in to the house. It was me that told him to

take the lid off. It was my fault, and now he was fighting
for his life and all I could do was pray.

I prayed like I had never prayed before! I prayed for
a miracle, for intervention, for a divine moment and touch
from God Himself. All I did was pray, pacing up and down
the halls of the hospital. I made deals with God. If He did
this, I would do that. If He did that, then I would do this.
You know, all the things that we do when we can't change
a situation.

My husband miraculously got healed. I remember
going to his hospital room and feeling the presence of God
as soon as I walked in. I even asked him, "Did you meet
God or something?" He told me that they had found the
infection and he was going to live. I was overjoyed with
emotion. My husband wasn't going to be taken from me.
We were going to live a long life. We were going to get
through this. We were going to be able to tell the testimony
of God's grace, love, and mercy upon us. This experience
was going to knit us as one, and we were going to grow old
together.

We had a long journey ahead. I was 25 years old
with four children and had gotten heavier. And now I had
scars on my legs, breasts that were skin grafted, and I
didn't think I looked very beautiful. My husband had scars
all over his chest, arms, and some of his face. We had to
learn a new normal.

When people say that they love a person
unconditionally, they never tell you the process that they
went through to get there. They didn't tell me about the
emotions that I would experience when I saw my husband
with his clothes off. Nobody told me how I was going to
feel as a woman looking in the mirror and seeing that my
breasts didn't look normal anymore.

They told me that these things could bring us
together, but they didn't tell me how long it would take.
They didn't tell me that sometimes I'd asked my husband

to just keep a shirt on so I didn't see the scars while he was making love to me. Nobody told me that I would struggle with taking my clothes off in front of my husband because I knew I didn't look beautiful anymore. I didn't know that, although we used to make love during the day before this happened, now we only would want to make love in the darkness of night.

Nobody told me I would struggle with self-worth. They didn't tell me how long the journey to acceptance was. So I made a lot of mistakes and said things that I wish I could take back. I hid from the things that I used to experience. My relationship and marriage were changing. Although I loved this man unconditionally, I was struggling with the sight of him and the sight of myself when I saw my reflection in the mirror. I wish I could go back and throw my clothes off as if it was no big deal and make love with my husband as if we had never seen or experienced trauma. But there was no going back in time to change what happened.

Even spending time with my rag doll couldn't take away this pain. There was no conversation that I could have with her that was going to convince me that I was beautiful or make me not see the scars on both of us. There wasn't a look that she could give me that would help me to grieve what we once had and now didn't. My rag doll used to bring me comfort, but now I couldn't even run to her. I had all of my emotions shut up inside of me, hoping that nobody would ever see what had happened and what I couldn't accept.

10

We continued trying to figure it all out and pretending the elephant in the room wasn't even there. Once again my husband was looking for another job, and so we were going to be moving. We packed up our stuff in boxes and headed to Delevan, New York where we rented a house on Marble Springs Road. It was a house that had just been renovated and was so pretty. Although it was kind of on the smaller side, it didn't matter because it was just so cute. It was nice having hardwood floors and really pretty carpet rather than old cabinets, mold, mice, or fleas.

We were settling further into our lives. I continued to homeschool the kids and enjoyed pretty much every moment of that. We fell into a routine, found a church that we really liked in Orchard Park, and started going there regularly. We sat in the second pew on the left-hand side. People would comment about our four pretty girls and how well behaved and respectful they were. We planned for special date nights together and had parents or aunts and uncles come over to babysit.

One weekend we had planned to go to the tractor pulls together at the Pike Fair. Something happened and I wasn't able to go, so I had no problem with my husband going by himself. I felt like we had come a long way and that I could trust him, so why shouldn't he go and have a good time? I didn't know that decision would affect the rest of my life. I had no idea the impact that decision would have on our family, on my children, and, once again, on my self-worth.

It was 21 days after that trip to the tractor pulls that my husband left again. He had met up with his old fling that had affected our engagement and marriage. Now I was away from everybody, living on top of a hill, and having to drive miles to even get to a store. I was shocked! I never ever thought that this would've happened again.

When the girls and I weren't home one day, he decided to sneak into the house through the window in the basement to collect all of his stuff. He put it all in garbage bags and shoved them out the window. When I found out, I had no words to put into a sentence as to how I was feeling. All I could do was get to church and cry at the altar, lifting my arms up in surrender, asking God to do a miracle.

My husband and I had a few conversations after that, but they did not bring forth reconciliation. He now was entangled in the relationship hook, line, and sinker. But I refused to give him a divorce. I was not willing to end what I believed God had put together. I went to church and marched around the sanctuary praying, believing, and standing upon the Word. I was not giving up that easy.

He continued on his path, and I continued on mine. We met one time at the railroad tracks near his job. I had lost a lot of weight and was now trying to live a better, healthier kind of lifestyle. But deep down inside it was mainly because I thought I would win him back. It had to be my fault that he had left! I couldn't keep my husband from running off again. My self-worth was shot.

When I got out of the car he was really surprised at how I looked and told me I was very pretty. After a little bit of small talk I asked him, "Are you coming back?" He told me that he had not signed up for having to be poor for the rest of his life, having to work really hard and not having a lot to show for it. He hated not having money in his wallet and wasn't going to live that way anymore. He had been promised this girl's family farm if we got a divorce.

My mind shut down, and I couldn't understand what I was hearing. He was going to give up his family, his wife and being a daddy because he wanted money in his wallet? That thought was all that kept running through my mind. I knew he was no longer the man I had married, but I was willing to fight for him at all costs.

For two years we went back and forth to court and I refused to give him a divorce. During those years New York was not a no-fault state. He had to prove why he wanted a divorce, and he had no evidence of me being a terrible person or wife. So I wasn't budging. I was going to stand my ground. I was going to speak to that mountain and that mountain was going to be removed and we were going to be a family that was not torn apart.

I wish I could have told myself all those years ago that God had a different plan and that I was going to be okay. I wish I would've known then that none of this actually had anything to do with me. There wasn't a single thing that I could've done to keep him happy and at home. I was so broken but yet so determined to continue to be faithful, to continue to thrive in my walk with Jesus.

By this time Josephine Priscilla sat on my dresser. I didn't have time to talk to her too much, and I really didn't know what to say to her anymore anyway. If she had been real, she could have told people so many stories about me. If the tears that fell upon her face could be bottled up, it would've been an ocean. But she wasn't real and couldn't help me, so I didn't grab her anymore. I just stared at her on my dresser.

The girls and I went to church three to four times a week. I couldn't get enough of the worship and presence of God. It kept me sane and hungry to do what was right. I met people that prayed with me, laid hands on me, and cried with me. They became my family! They took my daughters under their wings. It was a refreshing time in my life. Even though everything around me was falling apart, I felt God moving in my life. I was searching in the Bible all the time for verses that would lead me to answers God had for my life. I learned so much during those years. When I wasn't in church, I was building a sanctuary for my children and myself in my home. I would march around our house anointing every doorpost and doorway with oil. I stood upon the rock of Jesus and could not be moved.

During a Wednesday prayer meeting I saw a guy pacing up and down in the back of the church, praying. I remember thinking, "Wow, to have a guy pray that way is amazing to me!" It was something that I wasn't used to seeing. He was just lifting his hands to Heaven and praying. I thought, "I want that kind of guy in my life. When my husband comes back he's going to want to serve God the way that that man does."

I walked by him a couple of times, and by the third time he came near me. He told me that he was praying and asking God for a wife. God had told him to look up, and there I was walking past him. I had never heard anything like that before, and instead of laughing and telling this guy that he was a weirdo, I thought it was my awesome answer to prayer. God was going to bring a Godly man into my life, and here he was.

Until then, I had been convinced that I was probably going to be alone forever because I was standing on the Word of God to bring my husband back. But here God brought a different man, right in front of me, spoke to him and said I am to be his wife. I didn't think it was bizarre at all, so I embraced that and thanked God for this answer to my prayers. It was not the way I thought He was going to answer my prayers. But it seemed to me that it was the way that He chose to answer them.

We started a relationship, praying and talking about the word of God together. I was enthralled. The relationship started getting physically intimate, and I knew that I had somehow disappointed God. I cringed, wondering if His baseball bat was going to come out. The relationship was intense. Because I thought it was God's answer, I contacted my husband and told him we could get a divorce.

I look back to that moment now in such a different way. I see it as a lack of faith, perseverance, and obedience. I look at it as a time of shame. The relationship with this guy was so intense that I couldn't see the secrets that he was keeping and holding back from me. I just kept going, stepping one foot in front of the other, and that one foot in front of the other brought an end to my marriage. It brought an end to the dream of living happily ever after. As I looked into my daughters' eyes and saw the disappointment, I felt shame. I didn't keep my word to my children. I walked in my flesh because I couldn't see that this was not God's answer.

The relationship started unraveling after my divorce was final. There were secrets that were starting to come out, situations that I couldn't put my finger on but knew something was happening behind closed doors. I began to realize there was a problem. I didn't quite know what the problem was until this gentleman took me shopping and bought me a beautiful dress. It felt very significant because it made me feel beautiful. And people didn't buy me things. I was so in love at that moment because I thought I was somebody special. I thought I was worthy enough that somebody was willing to buy me something beautiful.

I wore the dress and then put it in his closet, only to find it was no longer there a week later. I couldn't understand where in the world the dress could be. When I asked, he told me he took it to the dry cleaners and forgot to pick it up. So I decided to go to the dry cleaners on my way home.

When I walked into the dry cleaners I heard an audible voice inside my spirit that said, "JCPenney's." When I went up to the counter and asked for my dress, they told me that there was no such dress there. I asked them to look again under a different name but to no avail. The dress was not there. I walked out of the dry cleaners wondering what the word JCPenney's meant.

When I drove back to his house and told him that I had gone to the dry cleaners, his face went as white as a ghost. I asked him again where the dress was, and he told me he had returned it back to JCPenney's because he needed the money. I was devastated and started to cry, not so much because of no longer having the dress but because it meant he didn't find me to be worthy enough to have the dress. I took it upon myself, blaming myself again for not being somebody that was worth something.

I ended the relationship that day. I walked away from the man that told me I was to be his wife. I walked away with the shame of ending my marriage, only to end up all alone. But I didn't know how to be alone. I didn't know how to stand up without falling down. I didn't know how to look into my daughters' eyes and see myself as their hero because I wasn't a hero in my own eyes. Everything was a mess, and nobody could help me with the dialogue that was happening inside of my head. I had disappointed God. And in disappointing God I didn't know where else to turn. That night I took my Josephine Priscilla off of my dresser and once again fell asleep with her in my arms.

11

The girls and I stepped back into our routine of life. I needed to focus on being a mom and meeting their needs. Sometimes I was so enthralled in my own feelings that I would forget that my children were also going through things and had their own. Their little minds couldn't figure out all that was going on with their mommy. I had to focus. I never wanted a moment of my children's lives to represent the hurt, pain, and rejection that I was feeling.

We needed to move again. The house we were living in was going to be sold. I wanted to move closer to our church anyway, so I began looking for apartments in Buffalo. I didn't know the area at all and had never lived in the city, so I didn't know what area to move into or stay away from. There was one apartment that, when we went to check out it out, the landlord showed up and said, "Ma'am this isn't the place for you. This isn't the area for you and your children." He suggested some streets in another area where I should look for an apartment for my little girls and myself.

I needed to be in church. They needed to be in church too. We needed family, and our church was that family. I needed to move as close as I could to this family that I longed for. We ended up finding a cute apartment right in South Buffalo, and I went to work creating the place into a home for my children and me.

We took in foster children, and my daughters liked that. I felt like I would make a difference in these foster kids' lives. I could offer some version of normalcy compared to the chaos of the home life that they had to endure. Many times the girls and I would be on the floor of the living room praying that God would continue to provide for our family while we tried to provide for others.

One thing I felt strongly that I wasn't supposed to waver on was homeschooling my children. Now that we were in the city, I wasn't as trusting as I would've been in a country school district. Also, homeschooling was an escape from the reality of my life. It was one area that I felt needed and like we were succeeding. I would lie up at night thinking of things that we could learn, places that we could go, and things that we could do. I felt like I had failed at so many things in my life that I couldn't fail at this. This was my accomplishment.

I made sure that the girls were in every kind of Christian class that I could get them in, ensuring that the Bible was the center of our lives. God was going to be proud of me, put the baseball bat back in the closet, and not have to use it on me ever again. I walked in faith, believed the impossible, and saw God move in our lives. I watched him provide for our needs.

I had opportunities to speak at a homeless shelter in the city, and my daughters had opportunities to sing. We would bake all day and then go to the shelter to minister to the women and children that made it their home. I taught Pioneer Girls in our church and made it fun. I was finding ways to have my life be used for the kingdom of God. Those were great moments.

Our church held an annual Fourth of July picnic/carnival. One year the girls and I were walking around playing the games, talking to people, and riding the ponies when this guy walked by. For some reason our eyes locked, and his brother told him that he needed to talk to me. So DJ came up to me and started a conversation. I'm not sure what the attraction was, but he was so funny and charismatic that flirting with him was fun. He walked away, and I thought that would be the end of it until he saw me again in church and started another conversation with me. DJ asked for my number, and I gave it to him. He called me that night and asked if we could go on a date on Thursday night. I said, "Sure."

DJ picked me up in his cargo truck. His daughter was with him, and I had to hold her on my lap as we drove to go listen to music at Thursday Night in the Square. Those were the early days when it wasn't very crowded and you could bring a blanket and sit and listen to music. His daughter never left my side. We had fun conversation and a great time. As we were walking back to his van, his daughter and I were walking ahead of him. He said, "You have a lot of walls up, and I will be the man that will knock them all down."

If only I would have just run away right there and never looked back. That statement haunted me for a very long time, as he ended up causing my walls to grow so far up to the sky that I didn't think even God could knock them down. We continued to talk on the phone, and I had him over for dinner for tacos for dinner one night with his daughter so she could meet all of my children. The girls got along really well, and his daughter was so excited to have "little sisters" that doted on her.

We continued to spend more time together, building a relationship. When it was time to meet his family I was shocked when I walked in the door and realized I knew his mom. She was a woman that I had prayed with in the kitchen of our church. Her wayward son needed to come back to God, and I needed to stand in agreement with her for my ex-husband. I was so surprised that the son that she was praying for that day was the one that I was dating now.

In the early days of our relationship DJ made me laugh and feel special. We got along really well. He played in a band, and when my daughters were at their father's I would go with him and sit and listen to him plays drums, sing, and then sometimes play guitar. I loved moments like that! He used to change the lyrics a little bit to "Brown Eyed Girl" and add my name to it. I felt really special!

We didn't have an intimate relationship right away because I did not want that to happen again. But the more time we spent together and the more we were alone, the more physical the relationship became. This progressed until one moment when we were intertwined with each other in my bedroom and had sex for the first time. I was so disappointed in myself. I wanted to be a testimony and example, but there I was, naked and having sex with someone that had just come back to the Lord.

Once we were intimate, the relationship took on a whole new meaning and I took on a whole new persona. Because we both had kids, and when we went out people thought we were a family, we began to start acting like one. He started spending more nights at my house even when he had his daughter. By that point I was cooking and cleaning for them both and putting gas in my car for both of our needs because he only had a cargo van. I was still a single mom with four children, but he didn't help me with food, gas, or outings.

Christmas was just around the corner, and we took the girls to chop down a tree so that his daughter could decorate one at our house. It was a lot of fun, and we did have a good time. On Christmas Eve the girls and I were invited over to his parents' house. We walked into the house and everybody was screaming at each other and I got kind of scared because I wasn't used to things like that. They were swearing and calling each other names. My brain didn't comprehend that Christians spoke that way.

I remember them then going into the living room, start hugging each other, speaking in tongues, praying, and asking each other for forgiveness. But then when they came back to the kitchen, they started screaming again. So I whispered to DJ, "I think it's time for the girls and me to go home. You can come to the house after you're done."

I put the girls in the car and we drove off. I was bewildered and kind of shaken up because I didn't know what all that really meant. He came to my house at two o'clock in the morning and then remembered the gifts that he had bought me. There was a can of Pringles and a calendar. I thought that was kind of weird and not very thoughtful for a significant other that you're spending your first Christmas with.

The girls had to go spend time at their dad's, so DJ and I spent the weekend together. It was weird not having my children around, and I was very sad. It was Christmas… how could I not have my children? We made love that night, and I thought he was a little more caring and thoughtful than usual. We lay in bed all the next morning just talking about life and where he thought this was headed. It gave me hope that our relationship could be like this on a regular basis.

That was not to be the case. Most of the time he kept me at an arm's distance. He would pull me in when he wanted to but then get some kind of attitude towards me, and I would have to try to figure him out. I felt like a yo-yo. One minute he was kind to me, the next he was passive, and then aggressive. I was always trying to get it right. I did a lot for him, and some of it was because I didn't want to lose him. I felt controlled by his behavior even then, never knowing when the light switch was going to go on or off.

My birthday came around, and nothing was really special. He didn't treat me like we were celebrating. I remember being sick! I didn't get sick very often, but lately my stomach was churning all the time. I was wondering why I didn't feel well, was dizzy all the time, and seemed to often have my head in the toilet. Many times I had to crawl from my bedroom to the bathroom because I was afraid that if I stood up I would fall back down.

This had been going on for three to four weeks when one of my friends asked me if I had taken a pregnancy test. That had never even crossed my mind! For some reason, in my brain, I thought since I wasn't married that I wasn't going to get pregnant. I was really naïve about that. So I decided to take a pregnancy test and couldn't believe my eyes when I looked down at the test and it said it was positive.

I was so scared at that very moment. I was ashamed and just wanted to hide. I remember looking around the room to make sure nobody else saw the pregnancy test even though I was all by myself. I didn't know how I could hide what I just found out. How in the world was I going to tell my children? How was I going to tell the parents of the Pioneer Girls that their unmarried teacher was now pregnant? How was I going to tell the pastor that I was pregnant when I was ushering every Sunday morning? And how was I going to tell my boyfriend??? My first thought, which breaks my heart today, was to not tell anybody. I never contemplated an abortion as a 16-year-old young girl but, as a-28-year old woman, my first thought was, "How can I end this without anyone knowing?" Somehow I felt God moving over to the closet to get His baseball bat. I was waiting for that bonk on my head because I was a naughty girl again.

I needed to gain my composure. I remember that I was shaking so badly that I needed to go for a walk. I needed to do something to wrap my brain around what I had done. How could a Christian woman that loves God, wants to serve Him, and so desperately just wants to be loved by Him end up pregnant? And how could this woman only have thoughts of an abortion as her way out?

It still makes me cry today as I think of those moments when I thought about taking a life because I was ashamed of mine. I can't believe that I thought the life growing inside of me wasn't worth giving a chance to because I was afraid of the stares from people in the church. I was afraid of the shame, snickers, and secrets behind my back. This was the first time that when I saw my rag doll sitting on my dresser, I actually threw her into my closet and shut the door. I couldn't even take her stares. I couldn't look into her eyes and see the disappointment.

When DJ came over a few days later, I asked him to take a walk with me. I had to tell him that I was pregnant. I didn't know whether I was just going to blurt it out, slide it into conversation, or talk around the mulberry bush and then end up just saying, "I'm pregnant." I remember doing all three!

The look on his face was one of dismay and disgust. He didn't put his arms around me or promise that we were going to be fine and would figure it out. He didn't look at me with a smile. There was no tenderness or affection. All I saw was shock. Then he looked at me and said, "I need to go home."

He did not speak to me for three weeks. At church, he sat on one side, and I sat on the other. He wouldn't speak to me at first. And then when he finally did, he said he hadn't signed up for this, had no intentions of marrying me, and that we would have to go to court to split our time with this child. I couldn't wrap my head around what he was saying and definitely couldn't imagine dividing my time with the baby growing inside of me. We went back and forth for a few weeks, and then finally he came back and said, "We'll figure it out." I felt like I was on a roller coaster. I didn't know then like I know now that I would *live* on that ride, never knowing if and when I would be at the top or bottom. He constantly kept me guessing and always thinking that I wasn't good enough.

I had to tell my daughters that I was pregnant. I didn't know how to tell them I had failed them and that I was sorry that my testimony as a Christian was flawed. Calling them into the living room, I asked them to sit down on the floor. I took a chair from the dining room, sat down in front of them, and told them I had to tell them something. They looked at me all confused, and a couple of them were worried. I said, "Mommy has some new. You may be happy or it might make you sad, but it's something that I need to tell you."

My daughters were ten and under, the youngest being five. As I looked into each one of their faces, tears started rolling down my face. I said, "Girls, I want you to know that Mommy is going to have a baby." My five year old little girl said, "I'm going to pray for twins. Mommy, can you have twins?" My oldest daughter said, "Well, I wish that when you got divorced that your body gets divorced and it doesn't want to feel love anymore because it would've made things a lot easier." I just laughed, as I couldn't believe the way she thought. My third daughter didn't say much. She was just very quiet. And my second little girl looked at me straight in the face and called me a hypocrite.

The shock and look of disappointment on her face absorbed all the way down to my bones. I didn't know whether to take her into my arms and hold her or just let her be. Her reaction was a hard pill to swallow, but I deserved it. I knew she was right! I had failed her. And even today, so many years later, I can still see her crushed face and broken heart. I wish I could've fixed it! I would spend years trying to. I think she has forgiven me but has not forgotten. She does now realize that I was human and, boy, does she adore her brothers. If there is one sister that loves them unconditionally, it is her. But I can remember that day as if it was yesterday, having to tell each one of them the truth… the truth that their mother was human, flawed, and imperfect.

12

You can only imagine my shock when I went for an ultrasound and was asked whether twins ran in our family or not. I said no, that I didn't know of any twins in my family. When the technician turned the screen towards me and said, "Well, there's twins now!" I could not believe it! I could not fathom that I was looking at two little babies growing inside of me. My brain just couldn't wrap its head around what was happening. My first thought was, "Wow, I thought of abortion. I would've killed one baby and still had another one growing inside of me." I had no intention of finding out the sex of the child (or children, for that matter) at that time but ended up finding out because of the measurements they were doing.

They told me I was going to have identical twin sons. That is a story all in itself. My whole life I had prayed that God would never give me boys. I never wanted to raise a child that would ever do what had been done to me. I wasn't confident enough that I could raise a son that would love his wife and never hurt any woman. And now here I was with two! God was doing something, but I didn't know what, and I didn't know if I was going to like it.

DJ and I had plans that evening to go out to dinner and open the envelope together to find out the sex of the baby. He picked me up, and I told him that due to extreme circumstances I had already found out what we were having. I had bought two blue carnations and had them and the manila envelope hiding in my hands when we got in the car. I asked him if he wanted to know or if he could guess what we were having. He said that he was having a son. I then took both carnations out from behind my back and said, "Make that two."

We drove in silence to the restaurant. He didn't open my car door for me. I had to walk across the street all by myself because he walked ahead of me. We sat down to eat dinner, and I tried to engage him in small talk, but he wouldn't speak to me. We finished dinner, got up, and left. Again he didn't walk beside me, and I had to get up into his truck by myself. He drove me home and did not say a word. I walked into my house, went to my room, and began to weep. I grabbed a blanket to hold and cry into, but there was no comfort in that. So I got up, went to the closet, and dug out my doll. I fell asleep in a puddle of my tears with her lying next to me catching them.

My heart was broken except for the fact that I was going to have twins and they were going to be twin boys. My long time dread was replaced with a knowing that if God was going to give me little boys to raise he was going to teach me *how* to raise them. Even if their father wasn't going to be around, I still was going to do my best. I started reading stories to them, putting on soft classical music, and laying my hands on my belly every night and praying. I thought about their lives and what I was willing to do to protect them. I was going to fight for them, make sure that nothing bad happened to them, and not let anyone harm them. Even if their dad didn't want anything to do with being with me, it was still going to be okay. I came to terms with the fact that I was going to be a single mother to six children.

He decided to come back into my life and said that maybe we should try and build this family. But he didn't help me much. He would come to my house and just let me cook and clean up after him. I still paid for all the food, and we drove my car filled with gas that I bought. But he was back, and I was going to find a way to make this work. It wasn't that I didn't love him. It was just that I didn't like the game of him loving me one minute and not the next or being treated like I was good one minute and the next receiving the silent treatment to punish me for something.

I was still really sick all the time. My pregnancies with the girls had been different, so this was a new experience for me. And, boy, did I get big! From behind you really couldn't tell I was pregnant… until I turned around. I was huge in the front and had to have a harness to lift up my belly. I was quite a sight.

His parents wouldn't speak to me and would even ignore me at church. They didn't come to the baby shower that was thrown for me. There was a lot of talk behind my back by this point, but I had too much on my plate to worry about it. I was blamed for everything and told that I was trapping their son.

We talked about marriage, but he wouldn't marry me until after the twins were born because he wanted me to prove I really loved him by getting my tubes tied. My whole life I had wanted as many children as possible, a quiver-full, enough to fill the pew of a church. But he looked at me as having trapped him. And so if I really loved him I would get my tubes tied.

To me that was a sin! I cried and went to the beach, down to the water's edge, to pray and ask God how I could do that. The Bible said that children were a blessing, an inheritance. Was I going to put an end to the possibility of ever having a child again because this man believed that I would give that up to prove I truly loved him, even when I believed that would be me disappointing God? I was so torn. If I didn't get my tubes tied and he broke up with me and chose not to marry me, then my newborn babies would be torn away from me and given to him every other weekend.

I really didn't feel like I had a choice. I knew it was his heart, not mine, that wanted my tubes tied. So in my mind he would be more accountable to God than me. I told him that if I did not have a ring on my finger, if we were not married before the twins were born, they were not going to have his last name. There was no response. I think maybe he thought I was kidding.

We didn't talk about it again until I went into premature labor. I was told dehydration had caused it and to be careful. They said I needed to be on bed rest, to not do any kind of strenuous jobs. How was I to rest though, with four children at home that I needed to take care of? He decided to move in, thinking that would help me. In actuality, it gave me more stress and things to do. But I was so stuck and desperate that I took any help that he was willing to give to me, even if it gave me more work in different ways.

The girls were getting excited about having babies in the house, and that added to my excitement. I picked out names after praying long and hard over their meanings. I had already started scrapbooking and journaling for each of them. Someday I would give both to them as gifts. I wrote them stories of what was going on, how I was feeling, and about little things from my past that maybe someday would be important to them.

I remember one day going to DJ's apartment building to go swimming because it was so hot. Being in the water was the only time that I felt any kind of relief because the twins were so heavy. I could barely walk, and when I did walk, I walked like a duck. I was planning my daughter's 10th birthday party. It was going to be a soccer party, and she was so excited that we were going to have it at a friend's house. She couldn't wait to have people over, get presents, and blow out her candles.

I decide… well actually, the twins decided that they wanted to enter this world the day before her birthday. I remember walking to the hospital because it was only around the corner. My mom met me there, and they immediately took me into a room because I was in full-blown labor. I was resting with my eyes closed, doing what I'd always done when I was in labor… just labor silently. I would focus on something as the labor pains were building up and keep that stare until the contractions ended. It worked for me.

When DJ came into the room, he immediately said, "Give her an epidural." I've never had one. I had delivered four babies naturally and planned to deliver these two like I had the others. He kept insisting on an epidural, and my mother said, "Just leave her alone. She really has done this before, and she'll get through this without having an epidural." He wouldn't shut up. I was getting angry, feeling like I was losing control of the birth of my children.

But I gave in because all I wanted was silence. I needed him to stop nagging, telling me what I was supposed to do with my body and my labor. The doctor came in with this big needle, and I had no idea what it was. It was the needle for the epidural. I was so angry and scared because I had never had one before. After they gave me the epidural, I couldn't feel anything anymore. I couldn't feel the movement or the tightness of my belly as it was contracting. Having no feeling was so foreign to me.

They rolled me into the delivery room and told me that I was ready. I'm glad they told me because, with not being able to feel anything, I had no idea. They had to tell me when to push, when to stop, and when to push again to move the babies' heads down farther. I remember feeling so disappointed that I couldn't feel the birth of my babies. Baby A came out, and they took him out of the room so I could deliver Baby B.

I didn't see them immediately after delivering them. Not getting to hold them right away left me feeling less accomplished than I had for the birth of my other children. I remember feeling robbed. I just needed to see and hold them! I remember wanting to immediately have my daughters come up to the hospital, and DJ told me that, no, they could see their brothers when we went home. The only one that was coming up would be his daughter since she didn't live with us. I was so angry, frustrated, and absolutely not in control.

But I was happy to have these beautiful little boys. I was so in love! My heart burst every time they put them in my arms. They taught me how to nurse two babies at once, but it felt like I was a milking machine instead of it being an intimate moment with my child. So, after I left the hospital, I never nursed both of them at the same time.

When I got home, my daughters were so excited to see their baby brothers! My oldest forgave me for giving birth right before her birthday. She forgave her brothers years later for messing up her special celebration. They were a better birthday present. My girls helped me immensely. They loved the twins so much and could not get enough of them. But I still struggled with the feeling that they were robbed of being able to see their brothers in the hospital.

After the boys were born we began looking for a house. We ended up buying one right down the road that we had first seen while walking around our neighborhood when I was still pregnant. It was a foreclosure, so DJ was able to get it for a really low price. And it would fit all of us. I ended up having to pack up my apartment, just after having twins, to move just down the street. I was recovering from carrying and birthing twins, had six children to care for, two of them nursing, and was getting no sleep. And now I was packing, moving, remodeling, and decorating a new house while preparing my mind to get my tubes tied. Looking at my two little boys as the last two children I would ever have was a lot, but, like always, I stepped up to the occasion and did what I was supposed to do.

13

After the sterilization I asked when we were going to get married. I was told to pick a date on the calendar and we would do it then. There was nothing romantic about it. I never got to experience a moment that took my breath away, where I had the opportunity to say, "Yes, I will be your wife." There were never bells ringing in my heart or a beating out of my chest.

We picked a day that he wasn't playing in his band and had off work, went to the courthouse in West Seneca, New York, and got married. There was no altar, no pretty décor, nothing. We got married in a random room full of boxes, all because he didn't want to be married in the church. I felt robbed again! But I guess I also deserved it.

It never really felt like a total lovebird kind of romance. There were some sweet and passionate instances when I felt loved and like I belonged. Looking, waiting, and longing for those scarce moments kept me married for as long as I was. But the sad truth is that the majority of the time I felt like I couldn't do anything right.

We fought a lot. There were times of peace when it was good, and then it was really good. But those moments never lasted. It seemed like we fought about literally everything, and neither one of us would give in to anything. For him, the way to shut me down was to call me names. I never realized that a man that said he loved me could call me so many nasty things. He would yell at me and demean me in front of my children. At first they were shocked and really didn't know what to say. After a while I felt like they got numb to it.

I tried really hard to do everything perfect and was always trying to figure out what that looked like. In the back of my head I always reminded myself that I couldn't keep a man around and that anything that happened would be my fault. He helped with the twins when people were around or there was a camera going. But for the most part the girls and I (really mostly the girls) took care of their brothers. My ex-husband paid $600 a month in child support. DJ gave me $400 of that to take care of the groceries and household needs of eight people, including two in diapers. I felt like I was shaking inside all the time because life with him wasn't at all like I had expected.

The fighting and bickering didn't stop, and four months into our marriage he hit me for the first time. My brain spiraled, unable to figure out what had just happened. I could not believe that a man had just hit me… and not with an open hand but with his fist into my shoulder. He said, "Maybe that will shut you up!" I just cried because I didn't know what else to do. I wondered at that moment if that was how my mom felt the first day that my dad hit her. Everything inside of me wanted to run, to take my children, get into a car, and run. But where was I going to run to? Who in the world was I going to tell that my Christian husband just punched me?

At that moment I thought back on when I went out to lunch with his ex-wife before we were married and her telling me about the domestic abuse that she went through with him, how he had grabbed her hair and dragged her. When she told me, I thought I was going to be different. He and I were going to have a different relationship. But when he hit me that first time, I knew we weren't.

DJ went upstairs, and I left him alone for some time. I don't know if it was out of fear, rage, and anger or just because I wanted him to feel really bad. When I walked up the stairs and into our bedroom, he was sitting on the bed with his hands over his head. He was actually crying. I sat by the bed next to him, and he told me he was sorry. He had promised himself that he would never hit me. He told me that wouldn't happen again, and I wish I hadn't believed him at that moment because it never stopped.

We would go in spurts of DJ being angry with me and then being very kind and then angry at me again. I never really knew what would set him off. I was somebody that wanted to talk, to solve problems right then and there rather than let them fester. But when he was angry he ignored me, pretended that I wasn't even around, as if I didn't exist. It was his way of making me pay for getting him mad. I never knew the moment that he was going to hit me. I never knew that one thing that would set him off. I lived on edge, trying to keep that part of our relationship a secret from my children, until I had to go to the hospital and came home with a sling for my shoulder. I couldn't hide the time that he pounded on me and left evident bruises. I knew that my daughters were catching on. Life was so out of control. I started getting migraines really bad but at the time had no idea what they were or why I got them. I didn't know that anxiety could cause those kinds of headaches. I went to the doctor for a checkup. He came in, sat down in front of me, and I asked, "What do you think is causing all of these headaches?" He told me that he felt I had *battered women syndrome*. I had thought I was really good at hiding what was going on in our home. But for some reason a doctor could see it on my face even though I wore a smile almost all the time and was happy. How could my secret be revealed outside of my home? I was so angry, not necessarily at the doctor, but I took it out on him. I told him to go to hell, that he didn't know anything. And I walked out of his office, never to return.

14

Whenever DJ got mad at me he would find something that was dear, that had meaning to me, and destroy it. One time he took all of my worship CDs and broke them in half in front of my children while saying, "This is what you do when a woman doesn't submit to you. You take something from her." I remember specifically another instance when I had prepared a big pan of lasagna for guests coming over. We got into an argument, I don't even remember over what. He walked to the refrigerator, got the lasagna out, and smashed it all over the floor. The pan broke and some of the kitchen floor tiles cracked.

He would spit in my face, tell me that I disgusted him and wasn't worth the breath that I breathed. Sometimes when he got angry he would make my sons sit on the couch and listen to him call me names. I was "white trash," "uneducated," a "whore," a "bitch"… anything that he could say to try and destroy my self-worth. One time he got so angry at me that he put his hands around my neck, started choking me, and told me that one way or another I was going to learn to submit. I don't remember how long I was passed out for, but when I woke up I was on the floor and he was sound asleep on the couch. It was as if he hadn't done anything, as if nothing had happened.

I really tried hard to not get him mad. I would go to church, sit in ladies' Bible studies, tell them what was going on in our home, and ask how I could make it better. People suggested that I go into the bathroom and pray, taking a pillow to scream into if I wanted to say something to him. I had others tell me to never deny him sex because that was "spiritual warfare" and that then, someday, he may no longer treat me the way that he did. I was told to try making his favorite meals and not talking to him right away but to just leave him alone for a while when he came home from work.

I was given lots of books to read about how to be a good wife, good servant, and good Christian even in a marriage where I felt unloved. I would read, pray, fast, and turn the worship music on really loud during the day to prepare my heart for whatever was going to happen when he walked in the door. But I always felt like he just wanted to fight, and he probably felt like I always wanted to fight. We were just not good with each other and very stubborn in our ways. Eventually we went to counseling several times and took a Married for Life class. For a while that helped. He began dealing with his inner self and, God was working on me too, peeling away at the layers of my brokenness.

Then something set him off. One Sunday he came home with a gift and handed it to me. Opening up the box, I saw the prettiest burgundy jumpsuit. I loved it and immediately put it on. We were on our way to go play tennis, so I couldn't wait to wear it! We got into our car, drove down the highway, and got into a huge argument. DJ told me that I wasn't appreciative of the gift that he gave to me and hadn't said "thank you."

I pulled over on the side of the road because I knew I had thanked him. He didn't care, and stopping the car just made him madder. He started pounding on me, pulling my hair, and wouldn't quit! I remember hearing horns beeping, but nobody stopped to help me. He was in such a rage that I had pulled over on the side of the road when we were supposed to be heading to tennis. Finally I was able to escape out of the car and away from his fists. He got into the driver's seat and just drove off.

I was crossing the highway so I could start walking home when a police car pulled over and asked me if I needed a ride. At the time I didn't feel like I had a choice but to get in his car because I thought it was illegal to be on the side of the road. I remember the police officer asked me what the red marks were on my neck. I don't remember what I told him. I just wanted to be quiet because I was afraid that if I said anything something would happen to me and my children would be taken away.

The officer drove me to my house. As I got out, he handed me a business card and said that I could call the number anytime I needed help. Whatever was going on, I needed to find a way to get away. I was so scared while I waited for DJ to get home. My nerves were about shot! But when he got home he didn't say a word. He just sat in his recliner and turned on the TV as if nothing had ever happened.

Another time we took a trip to Letchworth State Park to go on a canoeing excursion down the river. It was supposed to be a great date, and I was really excited because I had bought the canoe for him as a birthday present. When we got down to the river there wasn't a lot of water, and we were informed that we would probably have to carry our canoe in some spots. I had no idea how to row a canoe. I had no idea that left meant turning right and right meant turning left. And then, to top it all off, I was left-handed, so that added to my confusion. He was so mad at me!

At one point he fell out of the canoe, hurt his foot, and screamed at me even more than he already had been. I was so embarrassed because people were watching us. I could see the looks on their faces, as they felt sorry for me. He didn't care who was around or if people were staring. If he wanted to humiliate me, he was going to do it.

When the group stopped for a break, the owner of the excursion came over and told me that I could ride in his canoe with him. He informed DJ that he could ride by himself and then maybe that would calm the atmosphere. I got into the leader's canoe, and we started on down the river. He told me that if I didn't know how to row, it was okay, that I didn't need to. And if I wanted to learn, he would teach me very patiently.

He then looked at me and said, "I want to share something with you. I want to share the love of Jesus with you!" I couldn't help the tears from falling down my face, as this man thought I didn't know Jesus. I was so ashamed of what had happened with DJ on that river that made this man think we weren't Christians. I told him that I had accepted Jesus when I was 16 years old and that He was the only one that I could hang on to.   We were nearing the bank where we would get out and ride the bus back to headquarters. The leader secretly gave me a business card. It was his phone number and the number of a domestic violence hotline. My secret was out again on the Genesee River at Letchworth State Park! The secret that I was trying to hide within the four walls of my home was seeping into everything we did.

Where was my hope? Where was my Deliverer? And when was He coming? We got into the car in silence, drove home, and, as other incidences, this was never discussed again. When I got home I ran upstairs and grabbed Josephine off my dresser. How, as a thirtysomething-year-old woman, was a rag doll still my peace, my sense of calm in the midst of a storm?

15

I tried really hard to be a good mom, to find ways to contain how my marriage and homelife affected my children. I felt so short-fused all the time, like I was on edge, and I could see some of it in them. I needed to find a way to make all this anger go away. Whenever I went to our pastors, they told me to pray. I would have long conversations with my best friends, and we would fast together, hoping that God would intervene. Nothing seemed to help.

Family dinner time, with everyone together around the table, was something I always made sure that we had. One night the question was asked, "Who are everyone's top five favorite people?" Everybody went around the table, and when it got to DJ he said who his top three favorite people were. One of my daughters said, "Isn't Mommy one of your favorite people?" He told her I wasn't even one of his top ten. I was taken aback and felt so insulted in front of my children. How could he tell these girls that their mom wasn't one of his favorite people? But he just didn't care. It didn't bother him. He said he was just being honest. So I had to live with the thought, the concept, that I wasn't even close to being my husband's favorite person.

During the early years of our marriage I would go to yard sales to find Christmas presents for my kids because we didn't have any money. Well, to be specific, *I* didn't have any money. We had a checkbook, but I wasn't allowed to touch it, much less write a check for anything. So technically I knew where there was money, but it was always off-limits. And DJ wasn't very generous with buying things himself that were needed and would not give me any more than the $400 a month.

He was also very cautious with his own cash, counting it before he went to bed and again when he woke up in the morning. I would watch for any evenings that he didn't count it. Whenever I woke up during those nights, I'd pretend that I was going to the bathroom and silently crawl back into the room. I'd take the money off of his dresser, grab some of it, and hurriedly put the rest back. I thought that since he hadn't counted it beforehand he wouldn't know in the morning that I had taken any. Looking back now, I can't believe that I had to crawl around my bedroom, sneaking money from him while he was fast asleep, to put gas in my car or buy something for my kids or the house.

I began to find ways to make my own money. There was this place that did clinical research studies where they would test drugs. Participants were monitored while taking the drugs and then would get paid. I did that for a while and made pretty good money. But I couldn't do that forever because there were so many different criteria, so I wasn't always eligible to participate. I would also babysit other children so my kids could play soccer, be on the swim team, do things at church, and to buy school supplies.

I wanted to do something special for DJ for his 40th birthday, so I decided to make homemade spaghetti sauce and have his whole family over for dinner. Making the sauce was no easy ordeal, as it was something that simmered on the stove for days, and I worked hard on it. We got into an argument, and I got upset and went upstairs. I headed back downstairs when I heard some kind of slamming in the house and then his truck door slamming. When I walked into the kitchen, I saw that he had dumped the whole entire pot of spaghetti sauce into the sink. It was all over, splattered on the floor and counter.

He didn't come home for his birthday! The next morning I took a check out of the checkbook, went to the bank, and took money out to pay for all the ingredients that he had dumped down the drain. I was really scared and shaking by the time I got to the bank teller, but I was also so mad that he did that. In that moment I didn't even care about the consequences.

When DJ found out what I did, he changed the bank account, took my name off of it, and got a PO Box in the area where he worked every day. We had planned for the boys to be away so we could spend the weekend together. The girls had gone to their dad's, and I was going to go to work with DJ the next day. When he got home he pounded on me, pulling my hair and punching my back and arms to the point that I couldn't move. I ended up being the one that said I was sorry for what I did. There was never an apology from him.

The next morning not a word was spoken. I got into that truck with him and spent the whole day in total silence. I was in so much pain that I could barely get in and out of the truck. When I got home that evening I took my shirt off and saw that my whole body was black and blue. This rat race of a marriage, this dysfunction of a man, this home that was supposed to be built on solid ground, was truly on sinking sand. It was crumbling, and I had nowhere to turn, nowhere to go.

I called my brothers and asked if they could help me. They told me that they would come to our house and handle it, that they were willing to go to prison to do so but that I would need to leave DJ and never return. I didn't know if I could do that and asked if they could just come over, talk to and threaten him, and maybe that would work. My brothers told me again that if they came over it wasn't going to be just to talk. I told them I couldn't have that and then I stopped talking to them for a very long time.

DJ and I never talked about the incident. We just went about our lives as if everything had gone back to normal. We planned to go to the movies for my birthday, and I was told that I could pick any movie I wanted. My birthday is in the dead of winter, so it was cold, but I only had a leather jacket and some gloves. When we got to the movie theater, he picked a movie that he wanted to see. I told him it was my birthday and that I wanted to see another movie. He told me I was ungrateful, got into the car, and drove off without me.

What was I going to do in the middle of the theater parking lot with a husband that just drove off? Those were the days before cell phones, when you had to have quarters to call from a pay phone. I went into the theater, found the phone and I asked someone if I could borrow 50 cents. I called the only person whose number I remembered, one of DJ's cousins. They came to pick me up and dropped me off at my house. They didn't get out and didn't ask to come in. I thanked them for the ride and walked into the house.

The girls were at swimming lessons, so I knew they weren't going to be home. When I walked into the house, he was sitting in his recliner watching wrestling with not a care in the world. I took my purse, hit him hard in the face, and told him, "Don't you ever leave me, ever again, anywhere!" He got up off his chair, grabbed me by the back of my neck and threw me down to the floor. His nose was bleeding, but at that moment I didn't care. I was so angry that somebody that was supposed to love me had left me, on my birthday, in the middle of a parking lot, all because I wanted to watch a movie that he didn't.

There was a lot of screaming going on when the girls walked into the house. They saw DJ with his nose bleeding. He started packing his bags, and I immediately called our pastor to come over. When the pastor came, he sat down at the table and talked to my daughters. I sat outside because I was really scared that I had gone into a rage and hit DJ. The pastor came out of our house, looked at me straight in the face and said, "I'm really sorry for the situation. Someday, Bambi, you are going to be safe, and the secret that's going on within this house will be revealed. I will be praying for you." And he got into his car and drove off.

I didn't know if I was going to be safe going back into my house. But I thought since my daughters were there that I couldn't stay outside forever. DJ continued packing his bags and then drove off. At that very moment I didn't care. The only thing I cared about was that I had hit him and now I was going to be in big trouble. It didn't matter at that time how many times he had hit me, how many times I had been black and blue, how many times I had been assaulted. And it didn't even matter that he had left me. All that mattered now was that I had become the perpetrator and not the victim.

He was gone for a couple days, and then when he came back, he didn't speak to me. It's very difficult when you can sense the tension in the house and people aren't speaking to you. It's a weird atmosphere, an attitude in the house that you can't slice through or make it go away. This went on for weeks. He slept on the couch, and so every night I would hide my rag doll in my bed with me, thinking maybe she would keep me safe.

Finally one day I said, "What do I need to do to have you speak to me again?" He told me that I needed to sit the girls down, tell them I was sorry, and that I didn't know how to be a good submissive wife. I was to tell them that this whole incident was my fault and then he would talk to me. The girls came home from swim practice, and I asked them to sit on the couch. DJ was sitting in his recliner where he always was, and the girls sat down on the love seat. I was standing in the middle of the room between them. Looking at my daughters, I told them that I was sorry that they had to witness my anger and I wanted them to hear, in front of my husband, how sorry I was. I then looked over at DJ and said, "I'm sorry that I hit you with my purse and then was in a rage." I looked at my daughters and said that I needed to do a better job submitting and being a good wife.

My girls all looked at me like I was a foreign alien, and one of them looked very angry. I told them that I would do better. I had no idea that that moment, those words that he made me speak to my daughters, was going to change the course of my life forever. I could not imagine how that moment created a ripple effect, causing what was soon to happen. I didn't know at that time that I was entering the darkest season of my life.

16

DJ and I started attending a program held at a church in Buffalo. There, I examined the lies I had grown up believing that were contrary to the truth of who I was in Christ. It started to bring healing to my heart and soul. God was beginning to give me word pictures that revealed how He had been present and helped me during many traumatic moments throughout my life. The leaders of the program led me to pray and ask the Holy Spirit where He was during the moments I was being hit, insulted, taken advantage of or abused in some other way. I would sit and wait for God to speak to me. It was actually the best kind of counseling I have ever had. It brought life to my soul, showing me what a loving God I actually had. I didn't know then how much I was going to need that truth, as I would be falling into a dark hole.

One afternoon, when I got home from one of those sessions, the girls were all sitting in the living room. DJ was also there, sitting in his recliner. I was a little confused by the sobering atmosphere I walked into. My husband had actually been kind to me over the last few weeks. I felt a little more connection between us since a recent session where I was told that I needed to look at him as a seven-year-old little boy before I understood him as a man. I had begun to have compassion for him and we were in a good spot.

I remember asking, "What's going on?" I don't remember who first told me the news but I do remember that I blacked out when I heard it. Three of my girls were leaving and moving in with their dad. They didn't want to stay in their present environment. They would soon be packing up all their belongings, driving away, and not living in my home anymore.

Darkness fell over me and I began to experience the most agonizing pain in my heart. The turmoil in my mind felt like sinking into a black hole. I can still feel the trauma today, decades later. I couldn't breathe. I thought I was going to die! I know I wasn't literally going to die of a broken heart, but it felt like I was going to be put into a grave and buried, with dirt over top of me, never to feel truly alive ever again.

I went back to my counseling session and cried like I'd never cried before. The woman counselor held me as though I were a baby. I felt like a failure. I was worthless, abandoned, and betrayed. I saw myself as a perpetrator that had hurt precious cargo. I could not describe to anyone, or put into words, the darkness I was in.

The woman who was holding me continued to encourage me to pray for God to give me a word picture. I told her I didn't want to. I didn't care about a vision or what God was doing. All I wanted was for my babies, whom I had given birth to, held and protected all these years, to stay with me and not move in with their dad. I didn't want my children to have a life without me. I didn't want to wonder whether they would come over or not.

I remember getting down on the floor and curling up in a fetal position as if I was a baby in need of care. Rubbing my head and back, she said, "Just pray Bambi. Pray in the mist of the darkness and allow God to show you His light." I screamed, "God, what is the picture? What is your vision? What are you doing and why?" And I cried some more.

As I closed my eyes and tears ran down my face, God showed me three butterflies that were flying away. Those butterflies represented life, freedom, a new birth and beginning. Through all my tears, and all the agony my body was experiencing, I saw my three little girls through the eyes of God. Even though I didn't like it, even though it would cost me so much, I knew that God had a plan. I understood that my daughters could no longer walk through my turmoil. They needed to fly. The consequences of my life decisions had now cost me being able to live with my greatest treasures.

I got home from that session totally exhausted. I sat my girls down and told them I understood their decision but it could not be prolonged. I couldn't handle them staying around when I knew they were leaving. It wasn't something that I wanted to count down the days until, like anticipating a vacation. I decided that I wanted them gone before the boys' birthday.

In hindsight, it was probably the wrong decision to insist that, since they didn't want to be home, they couldn't be part of the twins' 5th birthday party. I know now that it shook up my daughters. They weren't leaving because they didn't love their little brothers. They were leaving because the pain of remaining in that home environment was too deep. But all I could do was think of my own pain of not living with them. I am sorry for that decision, and I wish I could go back and change some of those moments.

The day they were leaving, I remember telling them that I couldn't be there to watch. I got in my car and drove off. I didn't have the strength to witness my little girls getting into their dad's car, knowing they weren't coming back. After they left I came back, went into my bedroom, grabbed my rag doll, and cried myself to sleep.

I was never the same after that. It was as if darkness had overcome me and a knife of betrayal was piercing me in the back. I felt the agony of DJ's deception. The realization of what my covenant and marriage to him had cost me was overwhelming. *He* did this. *He* drove my daughters away. *He* took them from me.

My daughter Amber stayed back, and I tried to make life normal for her. But nothing was ever normal again. She picked up a lot of my slack around the house because I walked around in a fog. I wish I could go back and make things right for her, but by then I was too broken. I felt like every bone in my body didn't exist and my skin was just flopping around with nothing solid to hold it up. My body went through a huge change, reacting to the great depression and darkness, by going into early menopause. I never had a period again. Although I had my tubes tied already, my body now insured that I would never bear a child again.

Amber and I ended up arguing more often. I think I became extra possessive of her because I didn't want to lose her too. She was increasingly vocal to DJ, not putting up with his crap. That was good but also made things harder and more stressful.

One day when she and I got into an argument, I slapped her across the face. I was so angry, but what I really wanted was to hold her and beg her to never leave me. I wish I could go back and handle situations like that a whole lot better. I don't know whether it was later that day or if she waited until night, but Amber climbed out the window, drove off and didn't return. I eventually found her at her friend's house and asked her to come home. She said no. The next thing I knew, she wasn't at her friend's house anymore.

I called my mom and asked if she knew where Amber was because I had no idea where to even start looking. My mom said she didn't know. I continued to search for her, checking in with my mom several times. Nobody could find her. Come to find out, every time I called my mom, my daughter was sitting right there on the couch in her living room. Amber had made my mother's house her home.

The betrayal had begun again. How could my mom do that? How could she have had my daughter sitting right there and never told me? The betrayal would be hard to forgive. God would have to work with me over many years to let it go.

During the next several months I held Josephine often. She didn't quite bring comfort but did bring some semblance of security. She was the only thing in my life that wasn't taking something away from me but rather was always giving. She endured the pain with me, never telling me to move on or let it go. She knew that, in my own timing, I would one day be able to do that. But she never demanded it.

After the girls all left, my life shifted. They had done a lot with the twins, taking on the roles of second, third and fourth mommies to them. I never really had to worry before because the girls were always around, always protecting the boys. But now I was all by myself. I was the only one that could shield them from the things that were happening. Without the girls there to share in the truth of the abuse and secrets in our home, I alone bore the responsibility of making sure my boys were protected.

The name-calling got worse, as now DJ had another thing to use against me. What a terrible mom I was. I couldn't even keep my children, because they didn't want to be with me. He would never believe the truth, that it was him they didn't want to be around. He was too arrogant and narcissistic to look in the mirror and see his faults.

I went into overprotective mode, making sure that I did everything with my twins. My planned projects, our adventures and field trips, became even more extravagant. I searched for possible ways to connect with them and give them a healthy life.

DJ and I never stopped fighting. I felt like I was living in a war zone. Even when it wasn't physical abuse, it was still a war of words. My self-esteem was dwindling to zero.

17

I was so blessed, as I very much needed the friends God put in my life. They truly were my saving grace. I could tell them anything. They would pray with me and listen to me during days full of long conversations and constant crying.

I just wanted life as it was to stop, to change. I wanted the manipulation to cease in our household. DJ would say we were going out to ice cream, but then change his mind, after we all got in the car because I opened my mouth to say something. Then we all had to get out of the car, because he wasn't going anymore. And I had no money to just take them by myself.

If something broke in the house, DJ didn't care. It wasn't going to be fixed by him. There was a continual turnaround of vacuum cleaners, because I always had cheap ones that I was trying to fix and make last longer. If I didn't have one that was working, I had to use our shop vac to vacuum the living room. I would be on my hands and knees while he sat in his lounge chair watching. I felt like anything I did caused tension, and I tried to be away from him as much as possible. I also wanted my boys to be away from him and the constant arguing and name-calling.

One time DJ went golfing, and so the boys and I went to my girlfriend's house. She and I were playing tennis while her and my boys played together. I went to return a shot that she had volleyed to me, and I suddenly fell to the ground. I didn't know what I did, but I couldn't walk up her hill, and she had to drag me into her house. We called DJ, and he told me he would be there after he finished his game. It took both her husband and DJ to get me in the car, and he took me home. When we got there, he dragged me up the stairs and told me I would be fine. I was in so much excruciating pain, and my knee was swelling bigger and bigger. I asked if I could go to the hospital, and DJ told me there was no need. His sister called and asked if she could help out, but he said the boys and I would be fine.

The next morning, he went to work even though I could not move. I used my butt to get me to the bathroom, because I couldn't stand. I called my girlfriend, and she immediately came over to the house. She took the backseat out of her car and drove me to the hospital. I had broken my knee in three places and would eventually have to go to therapy. When we were done at the hospital, I called DJ and told him what happened.

He said I had to find a way to pay for it, and the best option was to sue my friend and her insurance company. I refused, and we had long fights over the fact that I would not sue one of my closest friend's homeowners insurance to pay for my medical bills and therapy. I had to gradually pay everything off myself and didn't go to therapy for very long because I didn't have the money.

In order to pay for my past medical bills and any essentials the boys and I needed, I just kept doing clinical research studies. Whenever I was at the clinic, I would call home to make sure the twins were being taken care of.

They would tell me that Daddy hadn't fed them. I'd be so angry that they were hungry and sitting on the couch watching baseball or golf all day instead of outside playing. After that happened a couple of times, I started having one of my friends take care of the twins so that I would always know they were being taken care of.

I saved up for a trip to go to Twinsburg where there was an annual festival for families that had twins. Being super excited about going, I would talk to DJ about coming, but he said it didn't interest him. I couldn't understand how doing a family trip was something he didn't want to do. I remember the twins asking him for some spending money, and he told them it wasn't his responsibility since he wasn't going.

I wasn't afraid to do things with just the three of us, and the boys and I had a blast. When I got back, DJ treated me so terribly, giving me the silent treatment because I dared to go and hadn't called him every minute that I was gone. That evening he slapped me and said, "Maybe you should think better than that next time."

DJ and I had planned a trip to Hawaii for our fifth wedding anniversary. As the departure date got closer, I started asking him if he was still going. He would tell me he wasn't, and I would cry and beg him to reconsider and go. I had never flown in a plane before, and I was really nervous to go by myself. He spit in my face and told me I wasn't someone he would want to go to Hawaii with and that he couldn't imagine having to listen to my voice for five days.

I went to Bible study and asked the women there what I should do. One of them suggested that I ask DJ if I could go by myself. When I got home, I asked him again if he was going to go. He said no and told me that he wouldn't be caught dead with me in Hawaii. I never thought I'd be brave enough to go on such a trip by myself or that he would agree to such a suggestion. But when I asked, he swore at me, essentially saying that he could care less.

I tried to arrange taking my daughter with me but she got a speeding ticket and wasn't able to go. However, she was willing to watch the boys while I was gone. DJ actually took me to the airport. I got on a plane for the very first time in my life, by myself, and flew nonstop 12 hours to Hawaii. I can't tell you what that trip did for me! It rebuilt my confidence, showing me that I was brave and strong. I talked to everybody that I could and met some amazing people.

I was sad when I had to get on the plane to go home, but I so missed my sons. I wanted to hug them and tell them how much their mommy loved them. DJ never wanted me to talk about the trip, as he didn't want to know anything about it. He did not care whether I had a good time or whether the trip sucked. And so, I never mentioned the trip to him.

Things were starting to get really bad between DJ and I. We couldn't be around each other and were fighting all the time. It was such a toxic relationship, but I felt like I had to stay. I was unable to face the possibility of him having my sons every other weekend and one day a week if we separated. I had to figure out a way for this to work and for my boys to be safe.

One evening we went to DJ's parents' house and were fighting. It was getting late, and I just wanted to go home. The boys had fallen asleep, and I decided to get ready to leave. Not thinking anything of it, I started the car as I buckled the first twin into his seat. I then went back inside, got the other one, and put him in the car too. DJ was still inside, so I walked back to the house to ask if he was coming. He started arguing with me again, so I said, "I'm just leaving."

When I got back outside, there was a police car in front of mine. I was a little bewildered, wondering what the police were doing there. He asked me whose car it was, and I said it was mine. He continued, "You have two little boys in there?" and I said, "Yes, I just put them in, turned the car on and went to get my husband and tell his parents that we were leaving."

By that time, DJ and his parents had come out of the house, because they saw the flashing lights through the window. The police officer asked again whose car that was, and DJ piped up and said, "It's hers. My van is down the street a little bit." The officer asked who had put the kids in the car, and my husband said, "She did." The policeman took handcuffs from the side of his waist, handcuffed me, and put me in the police car. He told me I was a reckless parent and that I was going to spend the night in jail.

I was so scared that I thought I might pee my pants. The last time I was in a police car was when I was 16 years old and had tried to take my life. I couldn't believe that my husband wasn't fighting for me, that he had allowed them to put me in the police car, shut the door, and tell me I had one phone call when I got to the station. The sick irony is that his brother-in-law was a police officer, and DJ, nor his parents, ever called him. They never made a phone call to get me out of the situation.

I was taken into the police station. People were snickering and talking behind my back, saying things like, "What a terrible mother! What kind of mother would leave her children in the car?" They gave me one phone call, so I called DJ and said, "You have to get me out of here!" He reminded me that I had been praying for God to use me and maybe this was the way. I just needed to look at it as a "Paul experience." I was crushed, ashamed, and embarrassed. At that moment I knew without a shadow of a doubt that this man hated me.

The officer put me in a cell with another woman. There was only a bench and a toilet. I was crying, and the other women in the surrounding cells began talking to me, asking what I had done. They told me that I could go to prison, was going to lose my children, and that the judge here wasn't lenient with stuff like that. The woman in my cell was really drunk. She peed on herself, cried, and told me a story about her daughter running away.

I didn't know what to do, and singing was the only thing I could think of. And so I sang every Sunday school song and hymn that I could remember. I sang quietly, and I sang loudly. I didn't stop singing or praying. If I had been home, I would have grabbed Josephine and let my tears fall on her ragged form. But there was no rag doll, nothing in my cell, to wipe away my tears. I sang as the tears flowed onto my cheeks, and I dabbed at them with my shirt.

I was brought back to the darkness, the reality, of losing my daughters. And now it felt like I was going to lose my sons. I didn't sleep. There was nowhere to lie down except the hard bench, and the cell smelled like urine because of the girl peeing in it and all over her clothes. It was really cold, both from the concrete and the atmosphere. But I felt that if I kept singing, maybe God would hear me and get me out of there.

In the morning we all received numbers and were told how we were going to go before the judge. I ended up being one of the last numbers called. When I stood in front of him, all I kept thinking and praying was, "Please! Mercy, mercy, mercy… and don't take my children away from me!"

The judge looked down at his paperwork and then told me he was sorry for what had happened. He was going to drop the case, and if nothing else happened within six months I wouldn't have to worry about it. I felt like a wind hit me, and I could have fallen to the ground. I couldn't believe my ears. The charges against me were dropped down to one misdemeanor.

I called DJ to come pick me up. He told me that he couldn't because he was out working and that I needed to call his father. I called his dad, and he came, picked me up and then brought my kids to my house. When DJ got home that evening, he nonchalantly asked me if I was okay. I told him that I would never again be okay. Now I knew the hate that he had for me, that he did not regard me as somebody important or precious.

To this day, whenever I hear a clinging of metal doors, it makes me jump. I can still remember the click of the lock of that cell. I will never forget the smell or the eeriness of that place. I will never forget being left alone there and told to use it as a "Paul experience." If I hadn't forgiven all that has happened, I know that this would have eaten me away by now. I have forgiven, but I will never forget.

I called my girlfriends again, told them what had happened and asked what I could do. I needed to do *something,* because I could not live this way for the rest of my life. What kind of justice was I giving to my sons? What kind of men would they grow up to be?

We decided to go on a fast and ask God for an opportunity that had nothing to do with me. We asked for something to happen that would make DJ's true colors stand out and I wouldn't be to blame. I prayed fervently, fasted, and believed that God would show up and do a miracle. I had no idea how it was going to work or what was He going to do, but I knew that He had to do something.

I was accepted into another clinical research study. I asked my daughter to come over for a weekend and watch the boys while I was gone. I didn't trust DJ with them, didn't trust that he would feed and properly care for them. After taking the twins out for the day, she brought them back home to feed them dinner and put them to bed. When she tried to take the boys upstairs to get ready for bed, DJ refused. He said he would do it and told the boys to sit down on the couch. He was watching wrestling. My daughter walked upstairs, huffing and puffing, because she was pretty upset.

A little while later she heard the boys crying downstairs and saying, "No Daddy, no Daddy!" She ran down to find the boys choking each other and DJ telling them that they could not stop until somebody tapped them out. My daughter was infuriated. She grabbed the boys, separated them and started screaming at my husband. Then she called the police on him. He was so angry with rage that he went up the stairs after her and hit her.

The police came to the house, talked to the boys, and told my daughter to take them away overnight until I could get back the next morning. Amber packed the boys an overnight bag and took them to my girlfriend's house. The police called me, asking if it was okay for my daughter to take my sons. I said, "Absolutely!" Then my daughter called and told me everything that was happening. I felt stuck, unable to leave the clinical research study because I needed the money so badly. But in hindsight, that was actually the beginning of an answered prayer. DJ's true colors had come out and it had nothing to do with me.

18

When I finally got out and home, things were missing from the house. All of DJ's clothes were gone, and he had taken furniture and other stuff. I went to the bank, but there was no money left in our account. As I was sitting at the bank, somebody told me to hurry up and take all the money that I could out of a credit card or I wasn't going to have any money. So I got a cash advance of $7,000. I didn't know how all of that worked, but I knew I had $7,000.

I got someone to come to the house and change the locks on my door. I didn't want to call DJ because at that moment I finally felt free of him! We made no contact for months. The boys and I just went about our lives. I continued to homeschool them. We would hang out in my room watching series like Little House on the Prairie and The Waltons. I would sit up at night reading books and especially the Word of God. It became alive to me, and I loved having Bible studies in our home. Life started to feel "normal," but this time without fear.

Our next-door neighbors adopted us into their family. We had campfires with them, and the boys would play over there and camp in their yard. The twins decided to join the Civil Air Patrol to prepare themselves for the military. I worked for a marketing company, wrote a unit study and tutored for a homeschooling family, babysat children in our home, stuffed envelopes, painted for friends, and eventually landed a job with the United States Census Bureau. I did anything I could do while still staying home to raise and homeschool my boys.

Finances were really tight, but we made it work. God met us, always providing in ways that we could have never imagined. I was able to save up enough money for us to go on a trip to Ohio, Kentucky, Alabama, and Texas. We made cookies for the boys to sell so that they could have spending money. Along the road, whenever possible, we stayed at friends' houses. And when we didn't, I just got a cheap motel. It was one of the best times that I'd ever had with my boys.

DJ ended up calling me while we were in Huntsville, Alabama at the Nassau Space Center. When my phone rang I answered but I wish I hadn't. He hadn't called in months and didn't ask about the boys. He said he would like to talk when I got back and was hoping that maybe we could work things out. I wanted so badly for my marriage to work because I viewed it as a covenant before God and I didn't want to fail again. But deep down inside I also just wanted God to do something to end it so that the pressure would be over. I didn't want to live on edge anymore, waiting for something to explode.

When the boys and I got home, DJ decided to come over. I remember they played a game with him where you put marbles on a damp tissue. The first person who made the tissue break when placing another marble on was the loser. I'm not sure why I remember that. We talked about him coming home, and he said he wanted to parent together. I didn't know at the time that his wanting to parent together was different from him wanting to be *husband and wife.* I would find that out over the next nine months of complete turmoil.

I felt a heaviness, an evil, had opened the door and entered our home. DJ slept on the couch instead of us sharing the same bed. He watched terrible horror movies that I would've never had in my home, didn't go to church with us, and never gave me a cent to take care of anything. It was like he was just there to torment my life. I tried everything I could to make sure that I was never home when he was and that the boys and I were always out doing something. We were always at an activity, a friend's house, the movies, or just out on an adventure.

The pipes burst at one of our rental properties, and when I told DJ about it, he said it was my responsibility and he wanted nothing to do with it. There were many times that we didn't have a lot of food in our house. He would buy his own food, leave it in his car, and wouldn't eat or share it with us. One time I even found his own private stash of toilet paper in his truck. He was bringing it into the house in the morning, going to the bathroom, and then taking it back out to his truck. He literally would not do anything to provide for us.

My sons began spending so much time playing at the neighbors that it became their second home, and the dad, their surrogate father. He took them to the movies, out for ice cream, and to his son's hockey games. One day when the twins had plans to go to a game, DJ wanted to take them to go get tires fixed on his van. I told him the boys didn't want to go because they were going to the hockey game. He started screaming, pushed me out of the way, and told me that he would be taking his sons with him. Running upstairs to where they were playing, he told the boys to get ready to leave with him. The twins started crying, told him, "No," and one of them ran out of the house. DJ picked up the other one, hoisted him up and over his shoulder and went to throw him into his van. He got free and ran to the neighbor's house instead.

That incident, that day, that moment in time was finally the end of all the abuse. That was the last day that he ever came into my home as my husband. That was the day that I knew that marriage was over. God had answered, but it would take another almost two years for the bondage and control that he had over me to fully come to an end.

The custody, court battles, reunification counseling, my attorney, the boys' attorney, the back-and-forth in the court room, and then finally a trial… a trial that would end this abuse. Finally a judge would say that we were free. It took two years, but in the end, DJ's true colors came out and the judge saw right through him.

The judge declared the divorce, looked at my now ex-husband, and told him that he would no longer be able to have my sons in a car with him or be with them alone. If he wanted to call or write them, he could do that. DJ had spent two years bringing me back and forth to court, but $30,000 later I was free! The truth had prevailed, and he could not torment me anymore. He would never again hit me, call me terrible names, or put my children in danger. He was no longer going to affect me or my life.

I was free to live again, free to believe again. I could look in the mirror, look at my life, and start becoming the woman that God had intended me to be. I no longer had to keep secrets about what was happening within the four walls of my home. The fear of something happening to my twins was gone. I was now free to be a mom. That was a good day! It felt so great to be able to go home, look at Josephine Priscilla, my forever present rag doll sitting on my dresser, and tell her I was now free.

Sometimes I think back to moments when it felt like DJ and I could have made it. There were times of laughter, of precious conversations, and a vulnerability that we had with each other when things were good. I think about the times I went to hear him play in the band and how he would just sweep me away. I remember deep talks about God and how, at different times, I felt God was moving in his life. Those moments don't take away the darkness, excuse behavior, or shut out the bad, but when I look at my two precious sons whom I love with all my heart, I thank him. The greatest joys of my life were birthed in the darkest of times.

There was no excuse for any of the abuse that took place in my marriage or home, but now it was time to start again. Now was the time to focus my life on raising two incredible boys to honor God and His kingdom. It was my responsibility now to lead them to truth, to teach them how men were really supposed to treat their wives. I was not going to be an easy parent, but I was going to help, guide, train, and direct my greatest joys, my whole life, my sons!

I took a break from dating or wanting to have any kind of relationship. I just focused on being a mom because I realized that I didn't have a long time left. The day would come quickly when they would be off by themselves, doing their own things and having their own families. And so we went on some really cool trips together, including riding in a covered wagon and up in a hot-air balloon. Any new experience that they wanted to try, I was up for it. I just wanted to enjoy parenting again.

We truly became like the Three Musketeers. I wouldn't find out until later that they were bothered by that, feeling like I depended on them too much. Maybe I did, but I loved them so much that, in my mind, that meant doing anything for them and wanting to give them the best life possible. I felt they had been robbed and I was to blame for some of that. They had experienced loss too, loss of a "mommy *and* daddy" home.

There was also the abandonment of their big sisters/surrogate mommies. And they lost years of a happy mom. I always felt like I was trying to make up for everything and could never get ahead of it. There wasn't much time left with them and yet so much I still wanted them to understand. I didn't want them to miss out on learning everything possible about life and having every opportunity.

My heart's desire was that they would grow up to be true men on the inside, and so I was always searching for opportunities for them to learn to be just that. I looked for men in the church and elsewhere that would be good examples but didn't find many after the divorce. It seemed like their friends' fathers, who had been part of their lives for years as they were growing up, now walked away from them. They turned their backs on my sons, as if we had some disease that they didn't want themselves or their children to catch. I was heartbroken by the rejection I felt my sons went through.

The twins wanted jobs early on in their teens. At 14 years old they got jobs with a contractor, working hard and for long hours. It was as if they had never wanted to be anything but men. By this time they were also interested in the military. It seemed like everything they did had to do with preparing for that life and getting ready for their careers in the army.

I didn't know how much I would miss them when they went because I was too busy preparing them. I was so focused on praying for them to be independent and responsible that I didn't realize I was parenting myself right out of a job. The only job that I had truly loved more than life itself was being their mom, and so I was not prepared for the day that they actually went to the recruiting office. I was even less prepared for being told that they could go into the military when they were 17. And I was not at all prepared that they would *want* to leave for the military at 17!

But conversations continued to center around just that... Conversations about how they were ready, how I had already raised men, and that they needed to go out into the world on their own without their mother chasing them. I didn't know the impact it would have on me. I didn't understand the emptiness I would feel. How could I be mad that they were leaving when that's what I had prepared them for? But yet I was! I was mad that there wasn't going to be people in my house laughing and planning to play tricks on people and setting up pranks.

My sons were so kind and very giving to me. One of them always wrote me poetry for Christmases and birthdays. And now they were men, telling me that they didn't need me but needed to go out into the world. I still tell them that if I had one regret in my life, it was letting them join the military at 17. I wish I could've had just one more year. But if I'm honest with myself, I don't think they would've survived another year being mothered and smothered by their mom. They were ready and I wasn't… but it wasn't about me.

Having an empty house was haunting to me. The quietness was deafening. Laughter was replaced with sorrow that drowned me. It was hard. Today, so many years later, it's still hard. But I know that I raised them and did my job. And they know that no matter how far away they are from me, I will always be in their corner. The house was quiet now. There was only me and Josephine, and she didn't leave my dresser too often. I didn't need her a lot during those years of raising my sons on my own and didn't know if I would ever really need her again. Time would tell…

Unlike the deep, strong relationships I had with my sons, those with my daughters was very limited and strained. There were times when they would come over and we all would really try to work on rebuilding, but it was never the same as before they left. When so many moments, so many years, are stolen, when you don't get to experience them together as mother and daughter, it's hard to start making time to make new moments a priority, much less build deeper connections. I have struggled a lot with having conversations and building those relationships. I don't know if it's really one person or another's fault, but because the relationships were taken away from me, I always feel like there is a conditional, rather than unconditional, love for me. Because the relationships have been so tainted, I find myself walking on eggshells, not always able to freely express my feelings about things. But

I can't go back and play the what-if game because life is how it is.

The older they have gotten and the longer they have navigated their own adult family dynamics, the more they understand the shoes I was walking in and the decisions I had to make. Whether they were right or wrong decisions, I had to make them. I lived with the consequences and paid deeply for every single one of those decisions. I wish I could go back and rebuild, not just for my sake, but also for how my decisions continue to have ripple effects throughout each of their lives and relationships.

I know I couldn't beg for them to stay, that day they told me they were leaving. I knew then that they had to and that they were making their own choices the same way I had been making mine. But I really don't think that their decision turned out exactly how they planned either. I wonder if we could have looked into a magic ball to see into the future if some of the decisions would have been made the way that they were.

In my heart, I still grieve how differently those relationships could have possibly turned out. I miss the chance to *really* be their mom. Our present day presumptions of what those adult mother-daughter relationships should be are based on unrealistic expectations. I know that. I don't know if any of us really understand what is normal to expect of the relationship between a mom and her daughters, and we have lost the chance to find out. Whether that chance was stolen from us or whether it just happened, we cannot change the past.

I surely always want them to know that a piece of my heart died that day and hasn't been brought back to life.

No matter where they are in life, no matter what they are doing, I love them so much! I am so proud of the people they have become! We will continue to work on our relationships. The older we get, the more we realize the time is short. Although we cannot make up for the past, we can surely develop a lasting relationship for the future. It may not look like it would have, should things have been different in the past, but it can be purposeful, unique, and ours.

19

As I said, I didn't date much after I had been through such a dramatic relationship, marriage, and divorce. I just wasn't interested. Maybe I had walls up, but at that time in my life I didn't even care. I was happy and wasn't lonely. There were times when a companion would have been nice, but I surely wasn't searching for one. Besides, I didn't have enough energy to go through that again. I had my friends, and those friendships were enough for me. They were people I could trust, laugh, cry, and dream with. Who needed a guy in their life when they had the best friends ever?

I didn't know that selling a phone would be something that would change my life. A cute guy saw that I was selling my phone on Facebook and decided to reach out to me. We started talking and laughed together. JP was a pastor. I personally thought I was too broken and tarnished to ever have a pastor even consider looking my way! But he seemed different. He said he was intrigued by me and wanted to get to know me. He wanted to be part of the passion I had for serving God, teaching the Word, and telling stories in a way that captivated anyone that was listening.

We decided, after weeks of talking, that we would meet in person and have a date. You have to remember, I wasn't looking to date anybody, but because JP loved the

Lord and was serving God as a pastor I was drawn to him. I was excited to meet a real godly man that was serving in ministry. We had a really nice date, considering that it was the first time we met.

JP was a little standoffish and kind of nerdy while I was more flamboyant and very much an extrovert. Because I knew he pastored a church, I had made assumptions and was surprised he didn't have more charisma. But due to my past experience in relationships with stronger personality men, I was okay with him being gentler. If I was going to allow somebody into my life, it had to be someone that wasn't going to try to take over that life. I was going to be me and nobody else but me.

We continued to date. He would let me read his sermons, and we prayed together over the phone. This brought me hope that this relationship would be different. But when I took JP around my friends, he seemed "off." They were concerned about the relationship and for me because they couldn't see what I saw in him. They felt like there were red flags but didn't know and couldn't pinpoint exactly what was wrong.

I had one girlfriend that loved and really encouraged the idea of my relationship with JP. Some of JP's family were also in ministry and had served in pastoral roles for a very long time at the church I had attended a while back. My friend and her husband attended that same church and had known his family there. So when they saw that there was a relationship developing, they encouraged it all the way. They felt that the two of us would make a dynamic team to minister to the community where JP's present church was located.

This was not JP's first experience pastoring. He and his first wife had started a church long ago that grew into a large ministry. But he had lost it all when they went through a nasty divorce. I couldn't figure out the details, as no one would talk about it openly or clearly. One detail I was told was that there was some kind of mental illness. I assumed that was in the past, felt like he deserved a chance, and thought his demeanor was just because he was shy.

Since all of my previous romantic relationships had become intimate too soon, I was determined that this time things were going to be done right. My friends always knew when I was with JP, and they had the right to contact me and ask what I was doing. Often times we were chaperoned because I wanted to make sure that the relationship was in right standing, that we didn't do anything in the flesh. I was surprised that that wasn't a priority to JP, and he didn't understand why we couldn't have a physical relationship. That caught me off guard since he was a pastor and preaching every Sunday. I personally thought it was just common sense that if you were leading a church then you needed to lead in righteousness. And if you weren't being righteous, how could you lead your church?

JP eventually understood that there was not going to be a physical relationship between us two, and became fine with that. I would drive to his place and he would come to mine, but we didn't spend a whole lot of time together in one setting. We had scheduled times to see each other, so I didn't see a lot of the things that I should have or would have seen if we were in many different settings and circumstances together. Part of why it ended up being that way was my own insecurity.

I struggled with knowing people were talking about me and forming an idea of the kind of person I was because I had already been married twice. Even though their thoughts and ideas were not based on truth, it still haunted me and made me feel tainted. I also believe I missed a lot of signals because I just didn't want to see them. I was very enticed by the fact that this relationship was leading me, a tainted woman, towards becoming not just a wife, but… a *pastor's wife*.

JP's parents loved me, and we would have long talks together. His father especially was funny and very kind to me. His children, however, did not like me. Church leaders and friends from his childhood and early ministry thought we were moving too fast. My friends thought he had mental illness. But his parents, siblings, current church members, and that one couple that I knew wanted us together, thinking I would be a great asset to both his well-being and his ministry.

I began to hear rumors about JP's mental illness and also mental illness within his extended family and specifically in his mom during his growing up years. People outside of my immediate circle started contacting me with concern. I just brushed off any red flags about him as being a symptom of him having gone through something traumatic and then losing everything. There was even a period of time when we couldn't talk on the phone because he thought people were listening to the phone calls. And we had to be careful where we talked in person because people were following him around. I had never dealt with mental illness, so I had no understanding of what he was talking about. I would brush it under the table or say, "Let's just confront these people," not understanding that *these people* were made up in his head.

Dear friends of mine invited us over. I was looking forward to getting their approval and was surprised when they didn't give it to me. My friend even wrote me a letter to tell me that, although JP seemed like a nice guy, he was not the nice guy for me. But I thought, since I had waited so long and hadn't jumped into relationships with just anyone, I knew what I was doing. It had been years since I had even considered being in a relationship, for goodness sake!

The relationship continued to progress until, on Easter, JP got down on one knee in front of his whole family and gave me a basket of plastic eggs to open. Every egg had something nice to say about me, a trait that I had, something about my personality, or something that he loved about me. The last egg had a ring in it, and then he asked me to marry him. With such a cute engagement, I was caught off guard and didn't think to say anything but yes! I was looking forward to a future as a dynamic couple that was going to travel the world teaching the gospel and spreading the good news.

A month after our engagement I heard that JP had hooked up with his ex-girlfriend. I just kind of laughed, thinking there was no way that it could be true. He had asked me to marry him and was leading a church. How could he have a relationship, or a one night fling, with his old girlfriend when he had just proposed to me? It felt like déjà vu, but how could this be happening to me again?

I didn't play nice this time. I was not going to fall for another man that would engage in an intimate relationship besides one with me. JP's father called and told me that I had every right to be upset but asked me to look at the bigger picture, at what God was really doing. He said God was doing something amazing in his son's life and I would see it if I could just stick it out! My other dear friends that were totally for us being together felt the same way.

I remember having so many conversations with my girlfriend about how some things were just weird, but I couldn't pinpoint anything. She would say that JP had been broken and now God had a plan for him. Like his father, she encouraged me that if I just stuck it out, I would see. I was told by others that if I could just be strong for him now and put my feelings aside he would be a dynamic husband.

Nobody in JP's court was telling me to run or considering my feelings about the whole situation. But I would have conversations with my friends late into the night, and we would go back and forth. I would make lists of why I should or shouldn't marry him, but ultimately, in the end, I wanted to love him back to wholeness. I wanted to be the woman that would care for him, that wouldn't run away. I made it all about him and thought God would take care of the rest.

We continued planning our wedding. I was excited about the ideas I had and how I was going to incorporate everything. It was going to be a Christ-centered marriage, and so the ceremony was going to represent the gospel. We were getting married in the fall. I bought pumpkins and was going to put scriptures on them. Our friends said that we could use their land. The festivities would end with a big campfire and s'mores in recognition of the fact that we had met at a campfire a long time before we got to know each other. It was going to be a beautiful fall day.

We chose to write our own vows. Friends were bringing dishes to pass, and we were supplying roast beef. My sons were going to give me away and were coming up with a song to rap. All my girls were going to be there. I even went wedding dress shopping.

We had an engagement party at one of my girlfriend's home. JP was supposed to go around to all of my friends asking questions about me so that he could get to know me even more. All of my girlfriends and friends said it was so awkward, that he wasn't good in crowds, and that he just talked like something was off. I really felt that God was going to take care of everything because this time around I was doing everything right. I was not having sex with a man that I was not married to, and to me that meant God was going to honor this relationship, this union.

20

The day before our wedding, the weather changed. It was going to be so cold that we were not going to be able to have it outside. My dear friends rented a big camp hall and everything had to be rearranged. We had to try contacting everybody through social media and text messages that the wedding had been changed to a different address.

The day of our wedding, my girls came to do my hair. My best friend came to support me and stand by my side. I had another close friend that was coming to lead us in worship during the ceremony. Everything was going to be perfect… except for the nudging in my spirit. Everything was as I had planned… except for the ache in my heart that wouldn't leave.

I ignored the feeling because I thought marrying JP was going to remove the shame, the cloud that was over me. I was no longer going to be a woman with a past, a mark. Now I would be a woman that shared a pulpit with her husband and brought others to Jesus. No matter what feelings of needing to run that I had inside me, they could not stop me from fulfilling this purpose.

I was spurred on by the promises of the people that knew him, that my being with him was going to make him better. I don't know if knowing the depth of his mental illness would have changed me walking down that aisle, with my sons on either sides of me. I don't know if any information that I was later given would have changed the moment that we said, "I do," and were pronounced husband and wife. I thought that maybe all the spinning questions going through my head weren't from God. Maybe my feelings and thoughts of confusion were caused by the darkness that didn't want us to bring light to the world. If that were the case, then I needed to, and was happy to, go through with this marriage.

We read our vows, promising all of these things to each other in front of our family and friends. Then we shared our first kiss as husband and wife and were introduced as Mr. and Mrs. At our reception, we had someone pray over our meal and other people that talked and gave blessings over our union. My daughter went around taking pictures, and others took our family photos. All the pictures were taken on her camera. But then we could not find it anywhere. My new husband and I went off to our honeymoon while my daughter kept searching for her camera with all the photos from our wedding day. But in the end, it had been stolen. I have an idea of who took it, but never told anyone.

When we got to the hotel room, I saw that JP had somebody come in and decorate it with a bouquet of roses in a vase and petals scattered about. There were also some snacks in a basket, and the bathtub was lined with candles. It was all really very cute! I could not wait to sink into a hot bathtub and just relax, as it had been a very long day. There were so many different emotions and thoughts running through my head, and I just needed to calm myself down.

As I was just beginning to settle in, JP asked how long I planned on being in the bathtub because I had made him wait a year to have sex with me. He wasn't laughing, and it wasn't something that he said to be cute. The look on his face showed that he was really serious. I realized that the relaxation I had so been looking forward to in the bathtub was not going to happen.

I got out and lay down in the bed next to him. Without creating any mood, without showing any emotional intimacy, he initiated sex. It felt so awkward and lasted all of five minutes. Afterward, he told me that it would get better but that this time he was just all excited. I lay there in complete disbelief. There had been no romance, no gentle touch or caressing of my face, no intimate moment of looking into each other's eyes. This was the first time that our bodies had been one with each other, and it was over in a moment. I wanted to cry. I needed to call home because that's where I wanted to be.

I called my daughter, and the first thing she said was, "Why are you calling? This is your honeymoon." I tried really hard to hold back the tears and said, "I just wanted to check up on everything." She told me that she could hear in my voice that something wasn't right. I told her I would be fine, loved everybody, and couldn't wait to see them soon. JP was oblivious to anything that was going on. My new husband that I was going to spend the rest of my life with didn't even notice the tears rolling down my face. All he wanted to know was that I was ready for a weekend full of sex.

We were gone for two days. During that time, I laid there for him over and over while he did his thing. It was never different than the first time and never lasted longer than five minutes. My body was getting sore, and I was struggling, as I had not been with a man for over six years. After the thirteenth time, I told him, "I cannot do this anymore!" He got really upset, and I ended up sleeping on the pullout couch. I felt dirty, as if he wouldn't even notice if I put a bag over my head. I had lain numb, unreactive, and it never crossed his mind to ask if I was okay. JP was my brand new husband, and yet I felt like a whore in the back seat of a car. Things did not get better. We ended up leaving early to go back home. I just wanted to be with my family. I missed them and the laughter in our home so badly.

We had decided as a couple that our schedule would be to spend half the week at my house in Buffalo and half the week at JP's church parsonage. He needed to preach, and I needed to be around his congregation. When it was time to stay at my house, he never stayed the full time. There was always an excuse why he couldn't be there. I understood that he probably wasn't very comfortable in my surroundings, as our household was always busy with people coming in and out. But he didn't even try to converse or mingle with anyone.

I felt like the only reason he was there was to have five minutes of sex, roll over, and go to sleep. He went to bed early, and then I would call my girlfriends and cry. I told them that I felt like it was just robotic. He didn't even know that *I* was there. Sometimes I would pull a blanket over my head and cry, and he never noticed.

There were other bizarre situations. He would stare at my window from outside, looking to see if anybody could see inside my house. He was always on edge and always needing to go to McDonald's or Burger King to get a Coke. When I went to the parsonage on the weekends, I would try to set up things for JP to do for the people in his church. He wanted me to preach a lot, but I would tell him that this was *his* church. I found a box of sermons. After asking him about it, I realized he was preaching word for word off of all the sermons he had preached years ago. I couldn't pinpoint everything that was going on but knew I could not live this way forever.

I loved the people in JP's church. Because it was such a small congregation, I thought it would be a good idea to send a card or visit with one of them each week. It was important to me to be making those connections. I had a vision in my mind of having the kind of parsonage that has an open-door policy. But every night that I was there, his only interest was to have sex with me that lasted five minutes and then fall asleep. I began wondering if there really was a mental illness, if something was drastically wrong. How could he have no other priorities and no emotion?

Our friends that had encouraged us to get married and encouraged me to just be there for him, that one day I would reap the benefits of helping my husband to be whole again, lived in the area. I would go over to their house and just cry, but they didn't seem to understand my predicament. I started looking through JP's kitchen medicine cabinet, taking pictures and sending them to one of my other friends that was a nurse. I was curious to see if she could figure out what kind of issues the medication was used for.

Thanksgiving and Christmas came and went. Finally, I just couldn't take it anymore. I called my nurse friend that I had given all JP's medication pictures to and asked if she'd found out anything. She said yes, that he was taking medication for paranoid schizophrenia. I was in total shock. I told her some of the things I was experiencing with him. She told me that they were normal symptoms for somebody with that kind of mental illness. All the pieces started coming together. He actually had no emotion for me. I knew at that moment that I needed to get out and get out fast. After everything I had already lived through, and at my age and stage of life, I was not willing to live like this.

I went back home to my house in Buffalo. The next time JP came over to see me, I confronted him. My friend was listening on the speakerphone of my cellphone, which I had hidden underneath my table. I asked JP, "Is there anything that you need to tell me? Anything that was necessary to tell me before we got married?" I wanted, needed, to know the truth.

JP was so angry. But I just kept asking, "What were you hiding from me?" He told me that his counselor had told him that he was on the mend and would be able to outgrow what was going on in his life. I asked him again, "What did you not tell me that I should've known before we got married?" I then decided to say, "I found your medication. I had one of my girlfriends who is a nurse look into what the medication was." I asked him point-blank, "Have you been diagnosed with paranoid schizophrenia?"

He told me that I had no right to look at his medications and that he had been on that before but his counselor said he didn't need it now. I told him, "You do not go on the mend with that mental illness. And how dare you not tell me, knowing that I had children and grandchildren in my life?!?" I was furious. I was even more furious at how I had been treated, like I was just an object to him. I realized that I was being used to help build his ministry while hiding what was going on inside of him.

His dad knew, his family knew, people around him knew, and nobody chose to tell me. But everything made sense after I found out the truth. When we were dating and he thought people were following him around, when he felt our phones were being tapped, he had been paranoid. The way he had been treating me, numb, without connection… it now made a lot of sense. I couldn't continue to live this way, in fear of what was going to come next or if anything would happen to my children.

I asked JP to leave. A few days later, when I knew he wouldn't be home, my son and I went to the parsonage. We filled my car with as much of my stuff as possible and then texted him to meet me at Burger King. I was already sitting down when he pulled up. He came into the restaurant and sat down across from me, looking hopeful that I was initiating getting back together. But there was no hope left in me, not for our relationship. I looked him straight in the face and said, "Don't you ever call me again. Don't you ever contact me. Don't you ever find me. Don't you ever approach me, ever again. Today it is over! You lied to me and I am ending it today." And then I got up and walked away!

At that moment I didn't care about the shame, the snickers, or what people were going to say. I didn't care how I was going to be treated when the word got out. I felt like I had been a pawn. I was used. Everybody from his circle that had been around me knew and had been hiding the secret. I don't know how I had the strength to do that and to just walk away. I just knew in my gut, in the innermost being of myself, that what I was feeling was real. How he had been treating me was real, and I wasn't going to tolerate that anymore from any man.

As I drove out of the parking lot from Burger King I had a realization. I had been so desperate to feel clean that I had overlooked so many signs, so many red flags… all because I didn't want to be tarnished goods anymore. I didn't want people to look at me and say, "Look, it's the woman that said she loved God but then was divorced two times!" Suddenly I could see the truth that I was just as guilty of using him as he was of using me. I had been so trapped and so deceived by my need to find worth in being the "preachers wife." I had been willing to throw away my actual self-worth just for a moment of being perceived by others as "clean." That deception had led me into a relationship that brought so much humiliation and pain. Now I had to face this present reality that we had used each other.

When I got back to my house, it's funny, but I didn't need my rag doll to help pick myself up off the floor. I didn't need her to allow me to cry. I didn't need to pick her up and hold her like a security blanket. I felt strong, but today the strength was not coming from having her. It was within me.

21

I believe that friendships are like brick and mortar. Everybody needs someone that has their back, someone who, if you're drowning, will jump in the water with a life preserver. I have been incredibly blessed by friendships that absolutely stick closer than a brother. My friends were like Josephine, my rag doll, but in human form. These women in my life have allowed me to be *me*. They have accepted the process that it has taken for me to become the person that I am today. They have brought quality to my life and looked at me through the eyes of my Heavenly Father. These were the women that were ready at any moment to be a listening ear, a shoulder to cry on, or to provide a bag of groceries. They were the ones that believed in me when I couldn't believe in myself.

The Bible says that if you find a good wife, she is more valuable even than a ruby. I would say that friendships are like that. As they are refined by going through fire together, they walk out as gold. That is worth the same as any precious jewel that you can wear on your fingers or around your neck. My friends walked with me through deep despair. They stuck up for me and didn't judge me. I could be real with them. They were women that allowed me to scream, cry, swear, and throw things. But after I was done, they also nursed me back to the truth of who I really am.

When a friendship is broken, it's kind of like the illustration of gluing two pieces of paper together. After they dry, if you try to rip them apart, they can never again be separated and returned to being individually fully intact. They will rip jagged with part of each piece of paper attached to the other one. That's how I felt when I lost some precious relationships. I felt like they took part of me with them. They took my secrets, my flaws, my heartache, the rawness of my life.

Those friendships had been the only stability in my life, and when they left or were taken away from me, it left me unable to function. Losing them left me feeling paralyzed, like I would never walk fully upright again. It was crippling because they were my crutches. Without them I was flimsy, going through the day afraid that I was going to fall and nobody would be there to catch me.

My friendships, my friends, became my family. I was loyal to them because they had been loyal to me. I would give anything to my friends because they had given all to me. But some of these women were stolen from me. There were husbands that were afraid that I was going to lead their wives astray. Others demanded that their wives not have a relationship with me because my personality was too strong.

I lost friendships because our political views differed. They chose to walk away instead of valuing and focusing on the things that we did have in common. I lost another friend that, even to this day, I don't understand why. It has burdened me with sorrow. At one time I thought nothing could break the friendships that have ended because the investment was so great in each other's lives.

I never looked for quantity of friends but always looked for quality. I wanted women that could speak into my life, would not allow me to be mediocre, and always encourage me to rise above any circumstance. When those friendships were lost and I suffered betrayal, it was hard because they were part of my identity. I looked at friends like a puzzle, each one of them a piece, and when everything was put in place, it created something amazing. So when I lost a piece, or it got stolen, the puzzle was not all together, and I didn't function like I did when the masterpiece was put together.

When I suffered great losses, those friendships had been my Josephine with skin on! When I spoke to Josephine she never answered back, but she did always bring comfort to me. My friendships were like that so when they were gone I was back speaking to a rag doll that brought me comfort but gave no answers. That's what happens when something that you love so dearly gets lost in the shuffle of life! Losing those relationships was a hard blow. It's something that's not easy to recover from, and it may be something I never will!

After the boys left for the military, the house became so deafeningly quiet that I needed to find a way to escape … maybe not to escape exactly, but I needed to deal with the emptiness. The company that I worked for offered me a position to travel 95% of the year. I trekked all over the country, visiting places that I only dreamed of going as a little girl… and possibly not even then because I didn't know that those places even existed.

I stayed in hotel rooms, worked really hard, and explored even harder. I can't even believe the things that I have been able to see and experience all across our country!

Sometimes I couldn't even believe that some of these places even existed. I've been blessed to have visited 42 out of the 50 states. I had to experience something significant in that state, or else I didn't add it to my list of states I've visited.

I paid off the rest of my legal fees, my house, and home equity loans. I was able to buy windows for every room in my house, give to others, and bless my children without needing to ask any questions. I knew that God was blessing me and giving me a piece of heaven in the travels that I experienced. I made the hotels that I stayed in my home by bringing things with me from my house. That way, when I walked in from a long day at work, I would see my things that comforted me, and I would feel "at home."

I took Josephine with me, not because I felt like I needed her but because she was a staple in my life. She was part of the foundation. She brought a sense of security. When I felt all alone, she was something that I was familiar with. So she always sat on the back of the couches in the little living rooms that were part of my hotel suites.

Traveling gave me the opportunity to see my children that were living in different parts of the country. I spent time with my son who was stationed in California, and we had so much fun experiencing so many awesome things together. I got to be part of my children's lives in ways that I wouldn't have had otherwise. I am so grateful for all of those moments and for the accomplishments that I have achieved in my life.

My exes thought I would never amount to anything, that I was just a low-class citizen, that dreams and opportunities would never come my way. I think they got fooled. They are the ones that missed out on the opportunities and on seeing me grow and develop into myself. I don't know if anything would've changed if they knew who I would become, who I am now. But that's not my concern. It's not my desire to even reflect on. And I know that I haven't been on this journey alone.

I found myself in a season that was full of transition. My many years of homeschooling life had come to an end. I began learning how to be the parent of all adult children. Everyone had left the nest and was moving on with their lives. They were building their own ways of doing things with their own families and creating their own traditions. There were career choices, weddings, and relocations across the country. The first of my grandchildren was born when I was just 40 years old, and thereafter it seemed like I was being blessed yearly with another one on the way.

My job kept me traveling most of the time. I was enjoying the fruits of my labor and learning for the first time what life was like outside of being a mom, wife, school teacher, and friend. Traveling gave me the opportunity to see my children and grandchildren that lived around the country more than I thought I would ever be able to visit them.

In 2018, all my children had their own plans for Christmas. No one was making a special trip to come home. With no one to stay home for or answer to, I planned a trip to go see the Grand Canyon and then decided to spend Christmas with my one son and his new bride. When I was with them, they gave me a gift that stated that there would be a special delivery. They were going to have their first child! It was a miracle that none of us thought could ever happen for them. I was so thrilled and couldn't wait to meet my beautiful grandbaby.

There were complications, and it wasn't an easy pregnancy. We were told by the doctor that if my daughter-in-love got to 24 weeks, they could take care of the rest. I never doubted for a moment that she would go to 24 weeks and that we would all be rejoicing. I would soon hold a new baby in my arms, a new grandchild in my heart.

On March 17, 2019 I received a text message from my son stating that my daughter-in-love was being rushed by helicopter to the hospital. I was in New York City, just getting ready to go on a carriage ride around Central Park and experience the history and beauty of the park. I didn't think anything of it. I knew she had gotten to 24 weeks, so I was just waiting for the news, the announcement, of the birth of my grandson.

I continued to enjoy my evening with one of my coworkers and periodically got little updates. One of the last updates was a text message from my son. He said that they thought this was going to be Isaac's lucky day, as he was going to meet Jesus. I was on my way back to my hotel when the text came through. It didn't register at all because I knew that she had gotten to 24 weeks.

I got back to my hotel room and was waiting for more news when I received a FaceTime call. It was from my precious daughter-in-love asking me if I wanted to meet my grandson. She showed me everything about sweet Isaac, describing every part of him. I saw his five little fingers and his beautiful face. She said she was going to show me last the thing that reminded her most of my son. She took the blanket off his feet, held them up in the air, and said, "See, Mom, he has his daddy's feet."

I tried to hold back the tears. I wanted to be strong. I didn't need her to see me weak, but my brain could not comprehend that my little grandson was going to take his last breath and then be placed in the arms of Jesus. I had never experienced a loss like that before. They were so many miles away. I was emptied out that day. The only thing I was left with was getting to see his perfect little body through this sacrifice of a mother that lost her son.

I didn't get a chance to hold him, kiss his forehead, and tell him how much Nona loved him. We would never get to play together, make crafts, or read a story. His little journal, the one that I was going to write letters to him in every time I went to his house, which I would then give him when he became a man, would never be written in. I never got to hug, congratulate, or then grieve with my son because we were so far apart.

The mommy and daddy were far away from everybody that day when, together, they kissed their little boy goodbye and mourned the loss of who he was but would never become. They mourned the dreams they had for him. We all mourned. We all were in shock. How could this have happened? How did we lose a little boy that none of us ever thought we were going to have? How do we all let go of our dreams of who he was going to be? I sat alone with all these emotions, all these thoughts. I was away from everybody. No one was there to hold me as I grieved the loss. I didn't know who to turn to as I was crumbling with thoughts of my grandson that was now gone.

Josephine didn't have to get me through any more traumas, but, because I had brought her from home to sit on the back of the couch in my hotel room, her presence was what got me through that night. She was the only familiar thing in my life at that moment. And I needed that as I mourned the death. As I scooped up and cradled her little rag-doll form, I was reminded of my daughter-in-love cradling her son. I thought about how I would forever be grateful for the moment that she gave me to see, to know, him. Such a sacrificial gift that, even in the middle of losing her child, she cared enough about me to introduce me to my grandson Isaac! I fell in love with that little boy that I was never going to physically hold. However, he will continue to impact my life and hold a place in my heart forever.

22

I had been traveling the majority of the time, and so, when I got home, the house was empty. My children's childhood home was now just empty walls full of memories of the past. The house was falling apart and I wasn't home long enough to even think about it or be willing to do anything about it. My neighbors had been looking after it and brought in my mail while I was gone. When I had time to stop in, I would check to make sure the pipes weren't frozen, that things were all turned off, and grab my stack of mail.

My children would ask me all the time what I planned on doing with the house. I never thought about letting it go because it was still my home. It was just empty and felt like an empty shell. Three out of my six children were living in the south and had informed me that there probably wasn't any chance that they were going to come back to Buffalo. So I often thought, "Why am I keeping this house?" It was probably because of the memories, it was paid for, and was mine. But I began to long for something more during the pandemic. I was spending most of my time in Kentucky, and in comparison, Buffalo's protocol was way too strict for me. I couldn't handle it. I needed the freedom to walk around in a store without a mask on without people staring at me. I didn't like feeling like my freedoms were being taken away from me. So I wasn't home very much even when I could be.

There was one time when I came home after it had been really windy. Some siding had partly fallen off the side of my house. It was dangling, and I didn't know when it was going to fall. That was the very moment I decided I was done. I don't know what it was about that specific moment or that specific thing. All I know is that was the moment I made a decision that I was leaving. I was getting rid of the house and moving south.

I walked in the door, looked around, and heard the laughter, giggles, and stories. I heard the prayer meetings and women's get-togethers. I heard the weeping, the fights, and the anger. And I heard love within those walls. There were stories of Christmas mornings and the games that we played as a family. Those walls reminded me of the "mouse trap game" where my children had to walk or run barefooted through 100 different mouse traps to get to a $100 bill on the table across the room. But those walls, and the memories they held, were not going to come back to life again, at least not for my family. They were now only the memories of the moments a family that used to live there had shared.

As I stood there and embraced that moment, it brought laughter, so much laughter. I walked around and saw all the women I'd invited to get together over the years, especially to gather at my table for elegant Christmas dinners. I reminisced about the conversations that we shared, and it brought a little tear that rolled down my cheek. I looked at the edges of every wall, seeing oil marks from the time I had marched around pleading the blood of Jesus and a hedge of protection over every entryway. I reached out and touched the stains that came from having used my finger to put anointing oil in every corner of that house.

I looked at the new windows that I had been able to afford after living with no windows that would open for seven years. My eyes roamed over the old furniture that had years of wear and tear. But it was *mine*, as I had bought and paid for it. I walked over to the piano, touched all the keys, and remembered my children sitting at this piano that a dear friend gave to me so we could have music back in our home. I looked out the front window that purposely had no curtain. If Jesus was walking the streets, I wanted him to be able to look inside my home and know that we were worshiping Him.

I sat at the dining room table remembering all the years of homeschooling my children right there. That table, that room, had been at the center of everything we did. I recalled the times of frustration and occasional anger while teaching when a child just wasn't getting it. I remembered all the crafts, projects, meals, games, and conversations.

I thought of the ginger ale that my sons and I made from scratch. We stuck it down in the basement until, a month later, there was a big bang when one of the bottles exploded. I looked out into the backyard and imagined the volleyball net up for family get-togethers at our Fourth of July picnics. I returned to the front window and let another tear fall down my face as I remembered the fireworks that had gotten better and better year after year. I thought of my sons spending hours rearranging their fireworks over and over again to make sure that the finale was always more amazing than the last time.

I walked upstairs to my room and looked at the Amish-built bedroom set that was bought for me. I continued to the bathroom, remembering the fights, the arguments, that took place while we were remodeling it. I went back into the hallway, looked down at the staircase, and remembered the long hours spent stripping the paint off of it to reveal the wood that had been painted over and over and over.

I looked outside the window that was at the foot of the stairs and saw my neighbor's house, my sons' second home. I felt the appreciation for their friendship well up in my heart, and more tears fell again. I reminisced about the protection they had provided my children, the campfires we had in their yard, the long conversations about politics, and the hideous Halloween decorations that they put out on October 31. I chuckled, thinking about how the neighborhood knew that we didn't celebrate that day and so the contrast between us always brought amusement and laughter within our community.

I went outside and looked at our garage where the snow got so high in 2008 that my sons could slide down the roof and into the snowbank. I remembered when our garage door was broken and it took he-man strength to open it. I thought about the boys calling me one day asking if they could keep some little mice that had made a home in a rug from our garage. My answer was, "Absolutely not, and get them out of there!"

I remembered the time that my sons were digging to China and my ex-husband couldn't figure out why I would ever let them dig a hole in our yard. I was always adventurous and wanted them to be allowed to explore. And so, if they thought they could get to China, who was I to tell them they couldn't? I laughed as I imagined the boys jumping the fences to play airsoft guns in the neighborhood and being called by the police because somebody thought there was a shooter in the area.

Oh the memories, oh the moments, oh the life that was lived in this home! Now it was time to say goodbye. As I was going through the things that had meant so much and called my children to see if they wanted those things that had been so dear to me, I was surprised they didn't want much. How could they not want their childhood things? How could they not want things to pass on to their children or to remember their own childhood? It was a huge reminder that we lived in a different time now and that those things didn't mean as much to them as they did to me.

My one daughter took the piano, as she had taught herself songs and would play for hours upon hours. It found a good place in her home, and hopefully her daughter will one day play for me. My second born daughter took the most, which made me feel good. Everybody says she's a lot like me, and her taking the things that she did confirmed that she was. When she and my grandchildren came over for the last time, it was heart-wrenching. I finally had a great relationship with my daughter, and my grandchildren thought I was amazing.

One of the last times that my grandchildren came over, I had my granddaughter put my make-up on me for the day. I couldn't go out in public the way that she did it, but I never told her that. I always tried to do crafts and other things with the little ones while they were at Nona's house. To know that these were going to be the last crafts they were going to do sitting at my dining room table made my heart ache. When my daughter packed up the things that she wanted and drove away that day, I know she had just as many tears falling down her face as I did.

I never felt that my decision was wrong or that I was doing something spontaneous. I just knew it was time. It doesn't mean that I don't miss Buffalo or my children's childhood home. But it does mean that I needed to make this decision and give myself a new start. This home held some amazing, great memories, but it also carried lots of sorrow, and it was time to start a fresh life.

After I packed the last box and said goodbye to one of my girlfriends that had come over, I placed Josephine in a secure box in the back of the car. We drove off toward another adventure with a new beginning and a fresh start. I was ready! Now Josephine and I would have a new place to live. But no matter where we ended up, as long as we were together, we were both *home*.

23

I get asked all the time why my mom named me Bambi. If I had a nickel for every time that question has been asked, I think I would be a billionaire. When I was a young girl I hated my name. I mean I *hated* it. I couldn't wait to get bigger so I could change it. For a lot of my life, I was determined that I was going to. Then I began to wonder, "What's in a name? Why is a person's name so important?" Even though a name becomes part of our identity, I found that I couldn't look at each one of my children and say, "Yes, they definitely are who I named them."

Names are important, however, and so every time somebody asks me about my name I have to tell them my story. There are many different accounts of how I got named Bambi as a newborn. My dad has one and my mom has another. But neither one really matters now. One of the stories was that my mother wanted to give me a name that would distract from anyone ever needing to ask my last name. My first name would be so unique that no one would have to ask, "Who?" because I would be the only Bambi in the room.

I heard another story that when I was born and first opened my eyes they were as big and beautiful as that of a deer. Then there was the one about my dad coming into the room drunk and wanting to see his son. When he was told that I was a daughter, he said he didn't want me. At that moment my eyes opened and my mom decided to give me a name that would leave a legacy because she knew I was going to have a hard life. There were other accounts of my name and about my birth. I think some of those stories will die with the people that are a part of them.

As a kid I was picked on all the time. I was made fun of and bullied because of my name. When I became a teenager, most guys weren't interested in taking me out or asking me to a school dance or prom, much less in being my boyfriend, because they were embarrassed to say they were with Bambi. As I got older, whenever I said my name, guys asked if that was my show name and if I was dancing somewhere that night. My ex-husbands made fun of my name and wouldn't introduce me unless they said "Bambi" with an accent.

My frustration grew over the years as I began to look in books of names but could never find the meaning of my name. So was I a child with no meaning? And was I still just a *nobody*? Did my name mean so little that not even the books liked it enough to give it a meaning? I remember asking my children if they would ever name their children after me, and the response was always, "No way!" I don't know if my children never liked my name or if it was just that they weren't going to name their child that name.

By the time I was in my early 30s I had just had it with my name. I wanted to have a conversation with God. Some of our greatest talks had been by water, so I decided to go to the beach. I just always felt His presence there, hearing the rolling of the water in the rushing of the waves. I sat down and started in on my monologue to God. I reminded Him of all the turmoil I had been through. I questioned if He had planned us all from the foundations of time and was the One that chose my name even before I was born. I challenged that if He knew the beginning from the end, then He knew what I was going to go through, experience, and how bullied I was going to get. I reminded Him, with tears falling down my face, that not even my ex-husband would call me by name.

I told him I had a better name and was going to call myself Janet. I don't know where Janet came from but always thought that if I changed my name, that's what it would be. So I decided to give God an ultimatum (*but I don't recommend that to anybody*). On this particular day, however, I think God had grace for where I was in my life and was listening to my heart. I told him that when I was done with our conversation and left the beach, I was headed straight to the bookstore. I was going to grab one of the books of names and their meanings off the shelf, and, if my name wasn't in there, I was going to go to the court and file for a name change. I looked up to heaven and told him I was serious.

I got in my car, drove to Barnes & Noble, and went inside. Walking right over to the name books, I grabbed one off the shelf. I was a little hesitant at first because I had just given God an ultimatum. I was scared. What if my name wasn't in there again? Was I actually brave enough to change it? When I looked through the pages of the letter B, I could not believe my eyes. My name was staring me right in the face. My name was there, in black and white, on the pages of this book.

My name, Bambi, had a meaning. My name meant *"child." Child* … what a precious, endearing, soft name I had. I decided to go and find my middle name. To my surprise, Lynn stood out in big, bold letters too. And Lynn meant "*holy*." I had to sit down in a chair at the nearest table. Gulping, I tried to catch my breath. As I looked at the pages where my name was written, I realized that when my names are put together, it means "*holy child*."

God knew… and I began to weep! He knew every single time somebody said my name. He knew they were calling me *Holy Child*. It still gives me chills as I write this because I remember that day, that moment, vividly as if it was yesterday. For the first time in my life, I was embracing my name. I wrapped my arms around myself and hugged, telling myself that God knew all along what He was doing. From the beginning, it was His plan to call me His holy child.

I didn't have to wear my name as shame because there was no shame to my name! There was only hope. There was only a new beginning. There was only an unveiling of a person that had meaning, and that meaning continues to carry me on. Every day now I look in the mirror and see what God sees, what God saw before the foundations of time. God did name me that day! He named me His holy child. Josephine's face would no longer be wet with my tears due to the betrayal that I thought my name carried. She would no longer pay the consequence of my screaming in her face as I unleashed the hurt that my name had caused. Now she would know that my name… like hers… had meaning, and I was never going to be ashamed of it again.

Life reminds me of a puzzle with all its pieces thrown to the floor and scattered around. Piece by piece we put it together, thinking it's going to look like the picture on the box. As the puzzle comes together, we realize that although it doesn't look like the box at all, it's still a masterpiece. It's still something of beauty. That's how I look at my life. It's consisted of a bunch of pieces that I never thought would be in my box of life, but when they all came together it was me.

Stories are never written for the author but rather for the readers. The author has a story to tell, to share, while the reader has the anticipation of reading the words on the pages of the book. Our lives are not lived for us but for the people that come after us. Our story is their survival guide, an example of how somebody endured. Readers are given a do-over or a first aid kit. They can take from the life of the author and learn something... and maybe, just maybe, get guidance and help that the author never had.

I think about my story as a scene from a book that I read and then movie that I saw. There were two characters who went to a garden. The garden was a mess with lots of weeds to pull out, things to dig up, and others to replant. One character was disgusted by the mess while the other saw a plan and said to wait before making a judgement. Towards the end of the movie, the previously disgusted character went back to the garden and saw the beauty of how everything came together.

I believe our lives are like that. We think nothing is fitting and that our lives are a mess. But there is a plan. You readers of this book could look at my life and think, "How did she survive?" You could look at my life and feel bad about all the things that I went through. You could see my life and ask, "Why?" But I choose to look at my life through the eyes of the Master Planner, the Master Sculptor, and the Master Chef. I choose to see my life as a creation of the Master Gardener and the Master Painter. I choose to view my life as an architect would, with all the plans set on paper. But then when changes take place, he incorporates them to create something even grander.

As our lives are lived, there are a lot of twists and turns. There are a lot of going up hills and down hills, a lot of rainbows and thunderstorms. But there's always a plan. We may not be privy to it, but as it unfolds we can see the plan was for our good and everything was working out.

I look at my life as a path toward healing. From the foundations of time, God had a plan for me. Some parts of it hurt me to the core. Others took my breath away and brought unstoppable tears. Sometimes His plans had me on the potter's wheel for what felt like way too long and in the fire longer than I anticipated. But the greatest treasures in life are those that experience a fire.

Life is all about choices and how we choose to take on every situation we experience. We can either turn it for good or let it destroy us and make us bitter. Every day I have to choose life, growth, and abundance. I know that the stories that have been written about me and the stories that I've been told were the stories that led me towards the path of forgiveness. I have the privilege to look in the mirror every morning and see an overcomer, a champion, a warrior, a woman who thrived. I see a woman with a story, and that story created a hero who is part of her reflection every day.

We all have so many obstacles in our life, but, if we choose to allow those obstacles to be lessons instead of something that defeats us, we learn that there is greater purpose for our lives. There is a greater design *if* we choose to allow the Creator to do His thing. I believe that God knew that a certain little girl, on a specific Christmas morning, was going to need this rag doll that she opened and that she would name her Josephine Priscilla after an orphan on the Oregon Trail.

God knew that six-year-old little girl was going to take a journey and it wasn't always going to be easy. But He gave her something, a gift and a treasure. This little rag doll was going to take a journey of a lifetime with a little girl. She was going to grow up with some horrific pain woven throughout her story. This is just as much Josephine's story as it is mine. Sometimes she was even the main character, as she brought healing to a broken girl and helped bring her back to life.

Resources

Suicide Hotline:

988

Domestic Violence Hotline:

1-800-799-7233

Author's Email:

Josephine.ourstory@gmail.com

Facebook Page:

The Journey of Josephine